To Karen,

ABE -vs- ADOLF

The True Story of
Holocaust Survivor Abe Peck

Wishing you best in all the your writing career!

✤ MAYA ROSS ✤

(a.k.a Maya)

WARNING: The material in this book contains graphic content and images which may be unsuitable for children or certain audiences. Reader discretion is advised.

ISBN: 978-0-99647-080-3

Library of Congress Control Number: 2016909832

TABLE OF CONTENTS

Preface

I first met Abe Peck a few years ago while I was volunteering at Café Europa, a social program for Holocaust survivors sponsored by the non-profit agency, Jewish Family Services of North Jersey. I had never met a Holocaust survivor before, so on my very first day I didn't know quite what to expect.

In my own head, I had a vision of decrepit old people shuffling in, chins tucked low, haggard and homeless-looking. But I was in for an enormous surprise. Not only did the survivors come strolling in with their heads held high, they were immaculately dressed and full of spunk. The women wore fashionable clothes, tasteful make-up, their hair beautifully styled; the men donned nice dress shirts and slacks, many in tailored sport coats and blazers.

Everyone was extremely friendly and talkative, their attitudes upbeat and cheery. I enjoyed mingling with them and it didn't take too long before I realized that most had never had their stories told. Although I am a fiction writer, I felt compelled to help these incredible people tell their tales of survival and courage. The first gentleman whom I spoke with immediately rolled up his shirt sleeve, without my asking, to show me the tattoo he was branded with as a prisoner in Auschwitz.

There it was, displayed on his left forearm in half-inch tall, clear black numerals: 143450. I cringed when I saw it. I'd heard about these tattooed numbers borne by Holocaust survivors my entire life but had never seen one up close.

This gentleman tried to dismiss my obvious revulsion by pointing to his tattoo and saying, "No, this is a good thing. If I didn't have this number I'd be dead. It means I would have been sent to the gas chambers. I'm only here because of this number."

These remarkable words—demonstrating the extraordinary ability to put a positive spin on one of the most heinous acts in world history—were uttered by the amazing man who is the subject of this book: Abe Peck.

Indeed, Abe's inspirational outlook is nothing short of exceptional in light of the fact that he survived prolonged imprisonment by the Nazis from the start of World War II until the very end. For over five years, he endured more horror and agony than any human being should ever have to experience. Starting with his captivity in a ghetto at only fifteen years old, Abe managed to live through nine different Nazi camps, death marches, lengthy confinement in cattle cars, years of slave labor, starvation, brutality and torture. He did not see freedom again until he was over twenty years old, when he was finally liberated from a concentration camp in Germany by American soldiers.

Abe's native country of Poland had the highest Jewish death toll in Eastern Europe. Pre-WWII, Poland was home to approximately 3.5 million Jewish citizens. It is estimated that over 90% were murdered during the war. And because the Nazis aimed to wipe out the entire Jewish race, making a concerted effort to kill all the young, over a million Jewish children were killed in the Holocaust, and only a few thousand survived.

Abe is one of the few Jews from his hometown of Szadek, Poland, who did not perish under Adolf Hitler's regime. Before the war, there was a total population of 3,500 people in Szadek—of which approximately 500 (14%) were Jews. After the war, there were only 13 Jews left (2.5% of the original 500), including Abe.

The horrid reality is that almost all of Abe's family and friends were annihilated. Out of 90 people spanning three generations, only Abe and 6 of his cousins survived. 7 out of 90 (7.7%) is but a tiny fraction of an enormous family, which included: 2 sets of grandparents, his mother, father, sister, 14 aunts, 14 uncles and 54 cousins.

At present, Abe is the only living Jewish survivor from the entire town of Szadek.

Living in America today, a free country whose Constitution protects all citizens, it is hard to imagine a time and place where certain groups of people—like the Jews—had no rules, laws, rights or remedies to protect them. The Jewish population of Nazi Germany and German-occupied countries found themselves in a world where their property and possessions were stolen outright, their lives were taken on a whim without penalty, and cold-blooded murders were planned and executed on a massive scale.

As a global society, we have made tremendous advancements since the 1930s and '40s, but we have failed to advance at the most basic level—to tolerate one another's differences. In a world with so many cultures, ethnicities, and religions, it is more important than ever for each of us to tolerate others who look different, who come from different backgrounds and who step into different houses of worship. Everyone has a right to peacefully exist, and that right must be respected. We can either embrace each other's differences, or allow them to destroy us.

The chilling truth is that our fate hinges on learning from our past. The history of humankind is fraught with crimes, wars, and atrocities stemming from hatred and bigotry. The cycle of intolerance, discrimination, and murder cannot be broken unless we learn from the evils of other eras.

Unfortunately, too many teach their young to put down, hate and blame others for their problems. Too many instill in their offspring their own irrational hatred and biases, which perpetuate onto subsequent generations. The result: anti-Jewish indoctrination continues to be a major problem in today's world.

With the resurgence of antisemitism, it is more important than ever for people to remember what happened during the Holocaust. Abe Peck has ripped open deep, old, painful wounds to share his personal story of horror and tragedy because, in his words, "I went through this so no one else has to."

Abe's story will not only carry on his own legacy, but stands as a legacy to the six million whose voices will never be heard. Abe desperately wanted to survive the war so he could tell the world about the savage brutality and massive killing operations he had personally witnessed, which destroyed his family, his community, and millions of Jewish people. Every day that he was imprisoned he fought a personal battle against Adolf Hitler. It came down to Abe vs. Adolf: If Abe died at the hands of the Nazis, then Hitler would have won. If Abe lived, then he would have defeated a tyrant.

After five indescribably horrific years, Abe won his personal war by surviving. He foiled the Nazis' sinister plan—"The Final Solution to the Jewish Question"—to annihilate every European Jew and wipe out the entire Jewish population. He rose up from nothing—from subhuman status under the Third Reich—to become a very successful businessman, charitable figure, husband, father and grandfather, and he considers every one of his successes to be another nail in Hitler's coffin.

Seventy years after his liberation, Abe continues his mission of educating the world to his eyewitness accounts of Nazi atrocities. The miraculous few who survived are dwindling toward extinction and their stories must be told before they die with them.

As you read these words, there are too many people around the world who will tell you the Holocaust never happened. It is tragic enough that so many millions of innocent people lost their lives; it would be the ultimate tragedy if our memories of them were wiped away as well. The ugly truth can never be eradicated from our books, our minds, or our hearts.

It is Abe's hope that through his story people around the world will experience one of the darkest chapters in human history firsthand and will never allow another Holocaust.

We must listen to Abe Peck. He speaks for millions.

*All statements contained in quotation marks throughout this work are the direct quotes of Abe Peck.

**All bracketed [ ] words have been added by the author to clarify Abe Peck's remarks. It is significant to note that English is Abe's fourth language, after Polish, Yiddish and German.*

Time Line of Abe Peck's Life

Born: November 25, 1924 in Szadek, Poland

German occupation of Szadek: September ,1939 [Abe 14 years old]

Szadek ghetto: May/June, 1940 to July, 1941 [Abe 15 to 16 years old]

Rawicz Working Camp: July, 1941 to August, 1943 (Abe's father died in Rawicz in Spring 1942) [Abe 16 to 18 years old]

Auschwitz/Birkenau: August, 1943 [Abe 18 years old]

Jaworzno: August, 1943 to January, 1945 [Abe 18 to 20 years old]

Death March from Auschwitz to Blechammer: January, 1945

Blechammer: Approximately January 20, 1945 to January 21, 1945

Gross-Rosen to Buchenwald: End of January, 1945 to February 10, 1945

Buchenwald to Natzweiler: February 10, 1945 to March 9, 1945

Natzweiler to Dachau: March 9, 1945 to April 7, 1945

Dachau to Allach: April 7, 1945 to April 12, 1945

Allach to Liberation: April 12, 1945 to April 30, 1945 [Abe 20 years old]

Marriage to survivor Helen Fajwelman: November 3, 1946 [Abe 21 years old]

Birth of Abe's son Jack: March 24, 1949 [Abe 24 years old]

Arrival in U.S.A.: September 30, 1949

Sworn in as U.S. citizen: October, 1955 [Abe 30 years old]

Purchased Home: October, 1956 [Abe 31 years old]

First trip to Israel: March, 1962 [Abe 38 years old]

Received high school diploma: 1964 [Abe 40 years old]

Founded JALEN custom upholstery business: October, 1969 [Abe 44 years old]

Retired: 1990 [Abe 65 years old]

Helen Died: March 12, 2005 [Abe 80 years old]

Returned to Poland: September, 2005

90th Birthday: November 25, 2014

CHAPTER 1

Childhood

On November 25, 1924, an innocent child was born to adoring parents who had no idea their lives were doomed. The little boy, Abraham Pik, was well-cared for, nurtured and protected by his loving family and close-knit community. Until his teenage years, he lived a simple, happy life, engaging in normal everyday activities. Bright, studious, athletic and kind, he was just a regular kid going about his regular life. When his world ultimately shattered around him, it wasn't because he had done anything wrong; his misfortune was being born in the wrong place at the wrong time.

Before World War II, Abe Pik[1] had what most people would consider to be a delightful childhood. Growing up in Poland in the small town of Szadek (pronounced *Shah-dek*), thirty-seven kilometers from the city of Lodz (pronounced *Loj*), Abe had many good friends and was blessed to be surrounded by a large doting family. He loved to learn and did extremely well in school. In his free time he enjoyed many outdoor activities such as boating and sledding.

Abe clearly remembers his summer and winter pursuits, describing them with vivid recall as though it were yesterday: "Me and my best friend Monick built a kayak. We bent thin plywood. There were no staples then—we used nails. We put tar on it. It had one oar. In the winter we had sleds."

He also has fond memories of swimming in a big lake near town—his father taught him how to swim—riding a bike—even though it was

_____

1 After World War II, Abe changed his surname to Peck

too big for him—and making his own telephone out of a shoe shine box and twine—which really worked!

"I was very happy."

Daily Life

Growing up in Szadek, Abe did not have the benefit of the modern amenities that we take for granted today. His day-to-day lifestyle was quite primitive, a far cry from our present-day world replete with computers, smartphones, cable television, video game systems, and the Internet.

There were no toilets inside Abe's home—they had to use an outhouse in the backyard. They had no running water—the water carrier would deliver their water in large buckets every day, sometimes twice a day. Baths were taken every second or third day in a round wooden tub with water warmed at the stove using wood and coal. The kitchen had no sink—they washed dishes in a special oval metal bin, similar to an oversized deep metal baking pan.

While the town of Szadek did have electric power in the 1930s, it was very limited. "There was only a few hours of electricity until 12 at night. At 11:30 p.m. the lights would blink and then shut off. People used lanterns outside. Inside, they used petroleum, called *nafta*, or candles."

Abe's family lived in a tiny home with only three rooms—a dining room, bedroom, and kitchen. His parents Hannah and Jacob slept in the bedroom while he and his sister Miriam shared the dining room. As Abe got older, his father hung a curtain across the dining room to give him and his sister more privacy.

During Abe's childhood, cars were a luxury item which only the wealthy could afford. Like the Pik family, most of the townspeople of Szadek were too poor to own cars and got around on horse and buggy. "There was only one taxi in town owned by a doctor. The motor needed to be hand-cranked and when it first started up, the kids would run faster than the car."

Abe explains the standard for being rich at that time: "Poland was a poor country. You were rich if your family ate meat two to three times a week. None of us were rich."

Getting food in Szadek wasn't as easy as running down to the local convenience store. Supermarkets did not exist and there were no grocery shops in town. To buy milk, people would make frequent trips to local farmers. Abe would go to a nearby farm every day or two toting a metal pail etched with one- and two-liter lines. "The farmer would milk the cow right into the pail. It had to be our pail to make sure it was kosher. My mother wasn't religious but kept a kosher house only so her brothers—who were very religious—could eat at our house."

Other dairy products like cheese, eggs and butter were purchased at a farmer's market in town every Wednesday. At the market, the Piks would also buy fresh fruit, vegetables, eggs, chickens, turkeys, ducks, and doves. In addition, Abe's father cultivated his own small garden in their yard. "My dad had planted green onions outside by the fence and would dump the dirty water on the vegetables."

Abe's father didn't just grow vegetables for his family's consumption. He owned a popular restaurant in town. "It was like a diner here. He served good things. We ate there once in a while. My father was an excellent cook. There was always turkey. People had dinner and lunch. We were not poor but not rich. We always had the necessities of life. I never remember going hungry to bed or not being clothed right."

Both of Abe's parents were intellectuals who stayed well-informed. "We had three or four newspapers every day. We had the *Folkstsaytung* [The People's Paper] in Yiddish, and the *Ekspres* in Polish, plus two weekly papers. Me and my sister couldn't wait to get the comics section from the Sunday papers."

Abe and his sister knew both Polish and Yiddish because they spoke Yiddish at home and learned Polish in school. Both his parents were fluent in Polish, Yiddish, and Russian, and his mother was also proficient in German.

Religious Observance

Although Abe was not brought up in a religious household, many of his parents' relatives from both sides of the family were devout followers of Judaism. His paternal grandfather, in particular, did not approve of Abe's father's lax attitude.

"Our house was not a strict religious house, but everyone went to *shul* [synagogue] on *Shabbos* [Sabbath]. I remember once when my father didn't go and after services at noon my grandfather came over and said, 'How come you didn't go?' He [my grandfather] didn't like his answer and smacked my father in the face, in front of me. He [my father] had shamed the family. My father apologized for it."

Abe's parents may not have been very religious—like other Jews who went to temple three times a day, seven days a week—but they celebrated Jewish holidays and kept up Jewish traditions. Passover, in particular, was a joyous holiday which everyone observed, no matter how religious. "My grandfather made sure there was a traditional Seder—he put on a white robe. The young people skipped a lot. We had two sets of dishes, Passover [and regular] dishes. Where I came from, even the most liberal person observed Passover. Maybe they didn't want to shame the family."

Abe regularly attended Hebrew School to study the Bible and learn prayers. "After school I went every day for one to one-and-a-half hours to *cheder* [religious school] which was at a Rebbi's [teacher's] house."

He also had a bar mitzvah, but it was not like any of the lavish affairs we see today. There were no DJs, dancers, or high-tech lighting. There was no ornate catering hall or extravagant smorgasbord topped off with a sundae bar and chocolate fountain. "In those days a bar mitzvah was very simple. The women made some food. There was *petcha* [called *jallia* in Yiddish, which is a cow's leg that becomes the consistency of gelatin when cooked] and herring."

Abe's preparation for his bar mitzvah service was also minimal. Nowadays, kids who are approaching bar mitzvah age study far in advance and lead large portions of the Sabbath service, but expectations were quite different back when Abe became a bar mitzvah.

"I had a bar mitzvah in 1938. We postponed it because of weather. I said maftir [the concluding portion of the Torah service on the Sabbath] for that particular week. The rabbi checked me out once or twice and that was the end of it."

Unfortunately, this otherwise happy occasion was overshadowed by the frightening predicament European Jews were facing at that juncture in history. Abe's sunny disposition instantly darkens when he discusses what it was like to be a Jew in pre-WWII Europe as antisemitism intensified.

"We heard Hitler's speeches on the radio. We got newspapers which reported what was happening in Germany. Hitler had been bad for Jews starting in 1933. He'd cleared very smart Jews from big and important positions in Germany. He'd made Jews close their businesses. It was a sad time. The Jewish people were depressed and worried at the time I became a bar mitzvah."

Antisemitism[2]

Long before Hitler's rise to power, antisemitism was always prevalent in Abe's life. Starting at a very young age, he was exposed to the cruelty, ignorance, and intolerance of others.

Even though Abe's parents were extraordinarily open-minded and free-thinking for their time, these admirable traits were not reflective of how others behaved. Abe reports that a deep-seated prejudice against Jews existed which made it difficult for him and his sister to befriend non-Jewish children. The majority of the non-Jewish townspeople were neither liberal nor tolerant like Abe's parents, and they passed their bias and hatred on to their children.

"In school we played games, like soccer, with non-Jewish kids but the Polish non-Jewish boys were antisemites. Outside of school, non-Jewish friends were few and far between because non-Jewish kids didn't want anyone to know if they were friends with Jews. I don't remember ever being invited to a non-Jewish home.

"When I was nine, ten, eleven, I remember the Poles used to have organizations [demonstrations] … very radical … antisemitic. They'd picket Jewish stores, 'Don't buy from a Jew!' 'Everybody to his own!' … all kinds of slogans. This was permitted by the government. A policeman would turn his head."

There was one specific holiday which Abe recalls was far worse for the Jewish population of Szadek than the usual daily antisemitic treatment they endured. From Abe's description, the celebration of this holiday was a precursor to the infamous *Kristallnacht*—the Night of Broken Glass—which occurred in Germany in 1938.

"They had a Catholic holiday—the Green Thursday [Maundy Thursday]. They [the townspeople] had a procession from their church.

---

2 The spelling "antisemitism"—as opposed to "anti-Semitism"—is used for the following reasons: First, the word itself is a misnomer in that it implies that it is directed at all Semitic people. Second, it is an artificial term invented by antisemites who wanted to provide their hatred against the Jewish people with a scientific-sounding justification (that is not grounded in biology). By highlighting "Semitism", it would give the term undeserved credibility.

No Jew could walk the streets. They'd throw stones and break the windows. Jewish stores would close shutters."

Although Abe experienced firsthand the unfair and inequitable treatment of bigoted people, he never understood it. The discrimination against Jews never made any sense to him—and still doesn't—as there was no rational basis for it. For instance, Abe recollects that when he was a child, a Jewish person wasn't permitted to own a farm.

"Jews couldn't do what a non-Jew could do even though they were very capable. There was a saying, 'A Jew can't be a farmer,' but a Jewish man was one of the most prosperous farmers around us. He couldn't [wasn't allowed to] own the land so he leased it."

As Abe grew, so did the hatred and intolerance of his Polish countrymen. By the late 1930s, the toxic atmosphere in Poland made conditions ripe for the Germans to step in and carry out their malevolent plans against the Jews.

"In 1939-40, those Poles became even more antisemitic. They agreed with the Germans—not about taking over Poland—but about what they were doing to the Jews. They used to squeal on us, [reporting] that some people had money or certain items the Germans wanted. Most of them were happy they were taking away the Jews' stores and property. They squealed so the Germans would search us and threaten us if we didn't give up our money."

School Photo of Abe at Age 5 or 6

Abe's mother's side: Uncle Kobel Najman & family
Only Abe's cousin Helen survived (bottom right corner)

Abe's father's sisters

Aunt Edith

Aunt Leiba Rifka

Aunt Hanna Hinda with husband
Frank Burakowski

Aunt Mindel

CHAPTER 2

School

Primary School

It was not easy for Jewish children to attend public school in Poland when Abe was a boy. Antisemitism was so pervasive during Abe's school-aged years that Jewish kids were regularly picked on and tormented. There were no rules or regulations protecting students against bullying like those we have in America today.

"In a class of thirty kids, there were five Jewish kids—three boys, two girls. In school we were always under threat of being hurt … beaten up. As a Jewish kid, the teachers didn't help."

In the hate-filled atmosphere Abe describes, Jewish students had to fend for themselves. He recounts the futile predicament of a Jewish child reporting to a teacher that a classmate had hurt him. "The teacher would say: '*You* must've done something!'"

For ethnic Poles, hatred of Jews was so ingrained that Abe believes antisemitism was being preached in church. He recites an expression that was used by the Jewish community when young Polish children exhibited signs of animosity toward their Jewish neighbors: "Polish kids already hate Jews when they drank their mother's milk."

Each day when Abe went to school, it was with the fear of being attacked. He had to find resourceful ways to ward off the brutal assaults of the Polish kids.

"I was not a big boy. I was a little guy. They would keep beating me up. In order not to get physically harmed I used to bribe the bullies in class by giving them things and doing their homework for them. I also had to bribe them—the antisemites—to have them stop another guy from beating me up."

Abe and his Jewish classmates were not only physically hurt, they were continually assailed with derogatory names by their peers. "They used to call us all kinds of names—like Christ killers."

He remembers being only seven years old when he was first accused of being a "Christ killer." Confused, he went home and asked his mother, "How can they say that I killed their God?" His mother replied, "You didn't kill him. They made up a story. They don't like us. I don't know why."

Although non-Jewish Polish parents may have taught their children to hate Jews, Abe's mother and father adopted a different approach. They did not raise their offspring to be disrespectful to, or contemptuous of, others.

"My parents instilled us with love and character, with strength of Jewish tradition and faith. But our secure world did not extend farther than the Jewish neighborhood. When a Jewish boy or girl would venture out they did encounter antisemitic jeers."

As if the constant threat of harm by his non-Jewish peers was not bad enough, Abe's early schooling was interrupted for one full year as the result of a bad accident. When he was only ten years old, he was at his grandmother's house chasing her cat when he inadvertently knocked a pot of boiling soup off the stove. The scalding liquid burned off all the skin on his lower right leg below the knee. There were no commercially available medicines for burns back then, so his mother and grandmother used plants and flowers grown in their garden to spread on his wounds and soothe him.

Due to this mishap, he needed to stay home to heal for an extended period of time. Although he did schoolwork at home, the public school would not give him credit, causing him to graduate one year late—in 1939.

After completing seven years of public school, from age five to thirteen, Abe was registered to go to high school—called *Gymnasium*—at the Yarachinsky School in the city of Lodz, about twenty miles from Szadek. It was too far for him to commute each day, so his parents arranged for him to live with an uncle.

Abe wanted to be a textile engineer, which required not only a high school degree, but a college education as well. In an era when people weaved their own garments at home, the textile trade was quite popular.

He was very much looking forward to the high school curriculum— math and language in the morning, engineering in the afternoon. "Study half a day, practice the craft half a day." His parents were sending him there even though they would have to cover the tuition costs. "High school wasn't free. You had to pay for it."

After high school his plan was to attend college in Belgium, similar to the path his mother had taken. "My mother had friends in Belgium. I was supposed to go there to college after I graduated and become a textile engineer."

If not for the German invasion and persecution of the Jews, Abe would have completed his education and lived a normal, happy life as a textile engineer in Poland. Once the war broke out, however, his high school and college degrees became unattainable. Despite his strong educational aspirations, his total schooling as a child was limited to only seven years.

Tragically, his educational pursuits morphed into a five-year grueling struggle to survive: first in a ghetto, then in nine different Nazi prison camps.

The ugly truth is that long before WWII, it was very hard for Jews in Poland to go to college. In fact, antisemitism was so strong in Poland that institutions of higher learning were almost exclusively reserved for non-Jews or those who were well-connected.

We take it for granted that in America today our colleges and universities are open to everyone, irrespective of gender, race, religion, or ethnic origin, but Abe tells us of a very different world— one where being the wrong religion was an automatic road block to advanced education, among other things.

"They wouldn't let Jews in. On applications, religion was required. If you put 'Jew' they wouldn't accept you. If Jews got degrees in Poland it was because they knew someone, like a senator."

To circumvent Poland's exclusion of the Jewish people from institutions of higher learning, Abe relates how in the large city of Lodz (which had 250,000 Jews), the Jews started their own colleges and universities. To staff the schools, they brought in professors from other countries.

Because Germany was far more progressive and enlightened than most of its neighbors prior to WWII, Abe believes that Germany was the least likely of the European countries to succumb to the radical beliefs of someone like Hitler. He states, "Germany was the most advanced country in Europe before the war. Germany was far more westernized and liberal at the time than Poland and the other countries … before Hitler's rise to power in 1933."

He adds, "Most parents would send their kids to college in Germany because they had the best teachers—better than in the U.S. And unlike Poland, Germany was open to educating Jewish students. I heard after the war that American teenagers had also been attending college in Germany."

Given what we now know about the barbaric reign of the Nazis, it is especially frightening to learn that such primitive, malevolent views took root and spread in a liberal democracy known for its technological and scientific innovations.

1) Tenzer
2) Abe Peck
3) Abe Unger
4) Esther Mittelman
5) Moniek Mast

6) Libel Granag
7) Joel Opatut
8) ?
9) ? } brother & sister
10) Polish Lady

School Class Photo (Abe is #2 in the back row)

CHAPTER 3

Family

As a young boy, Abe enjoyed his life in Szadek with his mother, father and older sister Miriam. They were part of a large loving community full of many friends and relatives.

Both of Abe's parents were bright, well-educated, active members of their town. When Abe speaks of them it is with the utmost regard, but there is always a sense of longing and pain which clouds his eyes. Clearly, at this point in his life his parents would have been long dead, but it is the horrific, senseless way in which they died that is always with him—along with the many years together of which he was robbed.

Abe's Father

Born in Szadek, Jacob Solomon (*Yakov Shlomo* in Yiddish) Pik was a veteran who fought for two countries in World War I. First, he served in the Russian army, and later, when Poland took over the region, in the Polish army. Abe possesses a handsome photo of his father dressed in his dark military uniform.

During Jacob Pik's tenure in the military, he was badly wounded. Fortunately, he did receive some recognition from Poland for his service to his country.

"Because he was a vet he got a concession—a liquor license. He was an invalid … he got shot in the arm. He was okay but you could see the bullet holes on his arm where the bullet went in and came out. When he'd raise his arms he'd show us that he could lift one arm higher than the other. With the liquor license, that's how he got the restaurant."

His father's restaurant was a small kosher establishment in town that catered to the Jewish population. Abe recalls that upon entering the restaurant, customers would use a big metal jar of water to wash their hands and say a prayer before eating.

In the summertime, Abe would help out in the restaurant making ice cream. "You put ice around a special barrel and turned the handle on top for about thirty minutes. Other kids helped out too. As payment, we would get vanilla or chocolate ice cream cones."

Besides running the restaurant, Abe's father was also a very athletic man. He coached a gymnastics team for Jewish children and was particularly passionate about soccer. Naturally, Abe played soccer too.

"My father wanted me to grow up to be a strong man. Do a lot of sports."

Jacob Pik was one of seven children—he had two younger brothers and four sisters (two older and two younger). All of his siblings—Abe's aunts and uncles—lived in Szadek and all were killed by Hitler.

Abe's father Jacob Pik (in the black jacket on the left)
coaching a gymnastics team

Jacob Pik in a military uniform (on right)

Abe's Mother

Hannah Najman (pronounced *Ny-man*) Pik was born in Lask, Poland, and had three older brothers, all extremely religious. One—Samuel (*Shmuel* in Hebrew)—was studying to be a rabbi in Slupsca; another—Machel—made religious hats in Szadek for the very observant; and the third—Abraham Yakov—was a businessman (a wholesale buyer/seller of grains) in Lodz. Abe was named after this third brother, Abraham, who died at a young age before Abe was born.

His mother's three brothers had a total of nineteen children. Tragically, after Hitler's slaughter of the Jewish people, only a tiny fraction remained.

Abe grimaces as he recites the pitiful statistic: "From each brother, only one child survived. Only three out of nineteen children."

Abe possesses only one photo of his mother taken in 1920 which was given to him by a great aunt—his grandmother's sister Yetka—whom he located in America by sheer luck after the war. In this aged photo, his mom sports a short haircut—very bold for that era—and dons a stylish scarf tied loosely around her neck.

Abe's mother was way ahead of her time in many ways. She transcended gender roles both in her extensive education as well as in the workplace, two areas traditionally reserved for males. While many women could not even read in this era, Hannah Pik had a career teaching. She would drop her kids off with her mother and head to her job.

"I admired my mother. She was an exceptional woman. My grandmother brought me up. She lived across the street. My mother would leave me with my grandmother and go to work. There were five or six grandkids my grandmother cared for.

"My mother would have loved to have lived in today's world when all women can get an education. She would always tell us how difficult it was to break away from her family and be independent. After public school, she wanted to go farther but her parents wouldn't let her. An aunt in Belgium took her in. There, she graduated college, then went back to Poland as a liberated woman and became a teacher. She was very, very educated. She taught German, Polish, and Russian in public schools and privately [as a tutor]. She also knew Yiddish and Hebrew. After she met my father, she moved to Szadek and they got married in 1920."

Hannah Pik instilled a positive learning atmosphere inside her own home. "We always had people coming into our house to have discussions. In our dining room we had two walls of books. I remember my mother cherished them. She made us [Abe and his sister] read *All Quiet on the Western Front*.

"My mother always praised me. Everything I did she said I'm doing good."

Abe's Mother Hannah Najman Pik

Abe's Parents

Hannah and Jacob Pik were exceptionally charitable and taught Abe and his sister at a young age about the importance of helping others. This benevolence stayed with Abe throughout his lifetime.

"They had plates on Yom Kippur to give charity to poor women and children without parents. My parents would lift me up to put money in each plate. Every Friday it was tradition to cook for Saturday. My mother would take a part of dinner and put on a special shawl and would go to give it to poor people. My father would joke, 'So who'd you give it to today?' My mother would say, 'For me to know and you to guess.' She never told anyone who she gave it to."

"My father helped poor people in a local organization like Jewish Family Services [a U.S.-based charity]. He volunteered and took me with him to show me to do something for people who needed help. He took me as a kid to change the straw-filled burlap mattresses that were in a house [a *Hachnosas Orchim*] for homeless people."

Perhaps the most notable aspect of the generosity of Abe's parents is that they routinely assisted others in need even though they were not rich themselves. Although they did not possess many valuables, they did have one item of great importance to Abe's mother.

"In our house there was a framed picture of Isaac Leib Peretz, the author of the book, *The Golden Chain* [a 1909 drama about the timeless chain of Jewish culture]. My mother got it as a wedding gift. It was a portrait of his chest and face created from Hebrew words in shades of ink. His eyes were darker and he had a twirly mustache. Written in Yiddish on it was 'The Golden Chain.' This was our most cherished thing in the house."

Years later, when Abe returned to Poland, he asked the few contemporaries who had remained in his hometown if they knew what had happened to this prized Peretz picture. Whether or not they were aware of the portrait's value, they claimed they had no knowledge of its whereabouts.

Abe's Siblings

Hannah and Jacob Pik had three children in total but their eldest— Abe's brother Hershel—died before Abe was born. Hershel was only two years old when he succumbed to a systemic infection resulting from a bad circumcision. Hershel, born in 1920, would have been four years older than Abe. Hannah and Jacob traveled all the way to Warsaw and Prague trying to help their first-born son, but to no avail. There is a small grave for Hershel in the Szadek cemetery.

Abe also had an older sister, Miriam, born in 1922. "My sister was very smart. She was smarter than me. She read a lot. She tutored kids in public school. My parents couldn't afford to send her to high school, which was expensive. She had an apprenticeship with an accountant at a bank.

"The accountant worked for free and my sister was a volunteer bookkeeper—similar to the accountants we have now. She also helped my mother. The bank was called The Hebrew Free Loan Association—*Gemilut Hesed* in Hebrew—meaning "bestowing kindness." My father was the president. Every town had a Hebrew Free Loan Association which would loan money to the poor—it was a charitable thing. People would have annual memberships and donate money. The bank loaned out the money with no interest and it was paid back. The Jewish law did not permit you to take interest on the money. It's written in the Bible."[3]

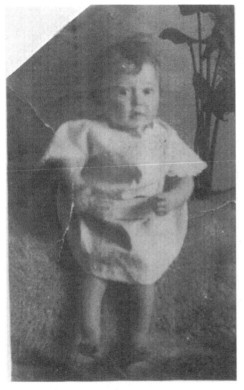

The only picture that exists of Abe's sister Miriam, Age 2

3 See The Five Books of Moses, translated by Evertt Fox, Schoken Books, 1983, Deuteronomy 23:20 "You are not to charge interest to your brother, interest in silver, interest in food, interest in anything for which you may charge interest."

Abe's father's parents: Pesa and Gedalia Hirsch

CHAPTER 4

The German Occupation

As soon as Adolf Hitler became Chancellor of Germany in 1933, European Jews were in trouble. By the late 1930s, Hitler's intense antisemitic propaganda had spread from Germany to surrounding countries the way a fire rages over all borders engulfing everything in its path. As Germany's power grew, so did its promulgation of anti-Jewish hatred.

"My family knew Hitler was terrible for the Jews. You could hear his speeches on the radio. My mother spoke German, and everybody in town understood. There were stories all over the papers about Hitler's speeches. He woke up antisemitism in Poland. He was preaching antisemitism and they liked him."

One of the ways Hitler built an enormous following was to pin the blame for Germany's loss in World War I, and the resultant economic problems, on the Jews. After World War I, under the 1919 Treaty of Versailles, Germany was forced to pay huge reparations, give up a significant portion of its land, and permanently reduce its army as punishment for its role in causing the war. In addition, foreign countries placed protective tariffs on German products. These punitive measures crippled Germany's economy, resulting in super inflation, massive unemployment, and fiscal collapse.

Hitler used the frightful social and economic conditions in Germany as a platform to blame the Jews even though Germany's economic devastation was the product of its defeat in World War I, the resulting penalties, and the Great Depression. As the Nazi regime restored economic stability to Germany, it gained the backing of the people. They bought into Hitler's revitalization plan, accepting his radical views and adopting his violent antisemitic methods.

When Hitler conquered other countries in Europe, he spread the same seeds of hatred that he had sowed in Germany. In Abe's assessment, the strong antisemitic climate in Poland primed the country for the Nazis' hateful policies and propaganda. He maintains that antisemitism was so prevalent in Poland that: "Polish people were happy to watch what was happening to the Jews. People that you went to school with, your neighbors, they laughed at you, like, 'Now you've got it. You deserve it!' You saw they were happy on their faces."

Abe offers us the firsthand perspective of a Polish Jew living through Hitler's exploitation of the European people and his sadistic Nazi campaign:

"They blamed everything on the Jews. If they didn't make enough money, have work, have a horse, they blamed it on the Jews. Hitler said Jews were all bankers and they're taking all the money. He was going to make Germany prosperous again.

"His first order of business was to get rid of the Jews. Hitler sent Polish Jews who had been living in Germany a long time back to Poland. In the early-to mid-30s, Germany passed laws that Jewish doctors couldn't practice, Jewish kids couldn't go to school, Jews couldn't own stores, factories….

"In school they were teaching kids not to have Jewish friends. Before that they [Jewish children] were assimilated. If a German family associated with a Jewish family they [the Nazis] harassed the German family too because they were Jewish lovers.

"Poland wasn't as bad as Germany at first. The older Jewish people thought [as conditions worsened], 'God's going to help us,' so only very few people left. Also, you needed money to leave."

The simple reality is that no one could have predicted the cold-blooded, systematic murdering of millions of innocent people. Even with the knowledge of the Holocaust we have today, it is still hard to accept that civilized societies could have committed such atrocities.

Abe shakes his head fiercely as he says, "Nobody in the world believed that there would be *Judenrein*, which means 'clean of Jews.'"

Fleeing Szadek

When World War II first started, set off by Germany's surprise attack on Poland on September 1, 1939, Abe was only fourteen years old. The German armies advanced so fast into Poland that the war was referred to as the *Blitzkrieg*—or "Lightning War."

It was only a matter of days before the Germans invaded Szadek. "We heard they were coming so fast. They were in motorized cars, jeeps, motorcycles, tanks ... in Poland we only had horses and buggies."

Abe's immediate family and grandparents tried to escape but were unsuccessful. The Piks were part of a contingent of forty to fifty people in about ten wagons who fled to Warsaw. They had relied upon propaganda they'd heard on the radio that the Polish army was strong and would fight off the Germans in Warsaw. "There was a saying in Polish: 'They [the Germans] are not even going to get a button off a Polish uniform!'"

Unfortunately, Abe's caravan never reached Warsaw. "I did not see it but we found out our rabbi was killed by a German bomb. A bomb hit his horse and buggy. We were part of that group on the way to Warsaw, running from the Germans. The Germans were coming from the west so we were running east. After a few days, they wouldn't let us into Warsaw because they said the Russians were coming from the east—so we headed home."

Was there any other place to which the Piks could have escaped?

"Once the war started we couldn't go anywhere. The Germans took over everything."

After the Nazis invaded Szadek, they allowed the Polish police to stay in place, but under their supervision. The Szadek Jews, however, were a different story.

"Their first order of business was to send all the Jews out of town because they determined Szadek was going to be part of the German Reich. They wanted the Jews to head farther south. We got on horses and buggies, got our possessions, some clothes and food, and we went to the first town which is Lask. We slept in our wagon for two to three days. In Lask, we were told we could bribe the SS men to get back into town."

The SS (an abbreviation for *Schutzstaffel*, meaning "Protection Squadron") was Hitler's elite paramilitary force that personally served as his ruthless henchmen. SS men swore their eternal faith and absolute loyalty to their *Führer* (meaning "leader," specifically Hitler) and were the formidable fighting force and military power of his Nazi regime. The SS, whose members believed they were racially superior, was responsible for the majority of war crimes committed under the Third Reich.

Once the SS had occupied the town of Szadek, its next interest was in seizing Jewish property and assets. *Zlotys*—Polish money—were not worth anything due to extreme inflation, so the townspeople of Szadek pooled together all of their gold and silver for an SS bribe so they would be allowed to return to their homes.

"We [Abe's family] gave silver candlesticks. People got all the gold in one pillowcase, silver in another, and they bribed the SS men. They let us back into town."

Unfortunately, while the Jewish citizens were gone, the non-Jews of Szadek had free reign to do whatever they pleased. When Abe's family and the other Szadek Jews returned to their town, they discovered that the majority of their homes had been looted by their neighbors.

"Most of our stuff was gone. Furniture…even pails to carry water… everything was taken."

Did Abe know who took his family's possessions?

"We would see our neighbors with our things, but there was nothing we could do about it. We were afraid they'd tell the Germans about us."

What was the trump card the neighbors held over Abe's family, in particular? The Piks had a dog named Hitler. Abe's father had gotten him from a farmer. They'd had the dog for about six years—since Adolf Hitler first came to power in Germany in1933. But the neighbors threatened to tell the German police that the family had a dog named Hitler, which most likely would not have been perceived in a positive light. The Piks were fearful the Germans would find out they had named their dog after the *Führer*.

"My mother didn't want Polish people to squeal on us so she kept saying, 'We have to get rid of the dog.' We were afraid if a neighbor told the Germans our dog was named Hitler they would hang us. They hanged people for less than that. Having a dog [named] Hitler was like a death sentence, for sure. But we loved our dog. We used to give away things to our neighbors so they wouldn't squeal on us.

"A few months after the war started we lost the dog. When we went to the ghetto [at] the beginning of 1940 we didn't have the dog anymore. I think my father gave him away to a farmer."

Abe recounts how during the German occupation many non-Jews tried to ingratiate themselves with the Nazis. Denouncing Jews was easy for those Poles who already disliked Jews before the Third Reich came to power. Abe says that if his Polish neighbors did not have any real incriminating information, they would fabricate some to get the Jews in trouble.

"They wanted to be nice to the Germans so they made up all kinds of stories." For instance, Abe recollects how neighbors would lie and report that Jews buried their valuables in their backyards.

Jews Were Targeted

Life under German Occupation rapidly deteriorated. The Jewish people, who had a long history of living peacefully amongst their friends and neighbors, were now dehumanized and persecuted solely because of their religion.

"We were guilty of the crime of the capital offense of being Jews."

As soon as the Germans occupied Szadek, the prospect of a normal life for Abe's family, and all the Jewish citizens of the town, was over. "Each day started with dread. Justice was no longer. The power of the law became the barrel of a gun. And out of all others, the Jews were singled out as targets of brutality and oppression for no other reason than having been born Jewish."

Does Abe know of any Jewish people who fought their German captors?

He steadfastly shakes his head. "They scared us. The first thing they did was hang a couple of people for no reason—just to show they could. It was to show that you don't have to commit a crime to be punished like that. The reason: You're Jewish. That's all."

The Nazis systematically carried out their plan to subjugate and ultimately eliminate the Jewish population of each town and city they occupied. One of the tactics they employed to avert an organized Jewish resistance was to disband whatever formal Jewish leadership existed at the time of their occupation.

"Every little town before the war had a Jewish local government elected. They ran Jewish affairs. When the Germans came in, they dissolved them."

Upon the Nazis' arrival in Szadek, to ensure there would be minimal resistance, they removed the biggest and strongest Jewish males from the outset.

"The first thing they [the Germans] did was take out the men. When they came into our town—and all the other towns—the first thing they did was to take out the leaders of the Jewish community ... killed them for no reason. They made something up like they didn't listen. They hanged ten men and all the Jewish people had to come out to the square to watch."

Laws Against The Jews

In Szadek, the Germans left most of the non-Jewish Polish citizens alone and allowed the Polish policemen to remain under their supervision, but enacted multiple decrees against the Jewish population. It didn't take long before Jewish citizens were stripped of their rights, their property, and their dignity. And it was nearly impossible for the Jewish people to escape.

"Jews couldn't move from the town without a permit. It was a crime for a Jew to leave the city. They'd be shot.

"Every day was another new law about Jews. The Germans figured out how to make you not a man—and they did it gradually.

"Right away the Jew became non-human. They treated us worse than a dog. We couldn't walk on the sidewalk–we had to walk in the streets. Sidewalks are not for Jews to walk.

"Right from the beginning Jews had to wear yellow Stars of David. We had to wear a yellow arm band. We had to put a yellow Star of David on our chest and back so we could be spotted from every direction, and if we were caught without it, the punishment was death.

"We had a curfew till 10:00 o'clock. They wouldn't let us go to shul on Saturday. Religious Jews snuck out to pray. There was an incident where they grabbed all the Jews in shul and took them outside and cut their beards with bayonets. Some of them they'd cut their chins off."

Abe personally witnessed a religious Jew with a long beard being assaulted by an SS officer. "He grabbed the beard and sliced it off with a bayonet. The man was bleeding."

Abe continues rattling off a long list of fearsome and appalling tactics the Nazis imposed on the Jewish citizens, along with all of the suffering that resulted:

"Jews could not be in commerce. Jews weren't allowed to own stores or be salesmen. They had to give away their stores to a non-Jew. Nobody would buy it when they would get it for free."

"Those who got first crack at the stores were of German descent but lived in Poland. They were *Volksdeutsche*—half German but Polish. They got priority. They would tell the Germans 'I want that store' and they'd chase the Jew out.

"My father closed his restaurant right away because he had no business. There were no more Jews coming to town.

"My mother wasn't allowed to teach. Jewish children weren't allowed to go to school. They [the Germans] changed the curriculum in the school.

"My sister worked as an accountant. The Germans came in and closed the bank."

Before the German Occupation, food had not been an issue. Abe explains, "We lived in a village. Food wasn't a problem. The big cities came to us for food."

But after the Germans took over, the Jewish people were starving. "It was hard to make a living. All the farmers around—we gave away almost everything for bread and soup. We were getting food by giving away things like a table, lamp, lantern, jewelry.

"They [the Germans] brought us down to such a point that some asked to be shot … killed. We became a thing, not a person. They treated us terribly. The way they did it was so tragic, so bad, it's hard to tell about it."*

Then, in May of 1940, the Germans' discriminatory laws reached a frightful climax when the Jewish residents of Szadek were struck with the most egregious decree: "All Jews have to pack and move into two streets."

It was further decreed that they were only allowed to take one bundle they could carry and a pot to cook with.

"We had only two to three hours to get out [of our homes]. You could only take what you could carry. Mattresses were bags filled with straw. I remember everyone carried a mattress and pots and pans. My family took clothes too."

Thus, after months of being tormented, persecuted, and starved in their own homes, the Jews of Szadek were forced into even worse conditions in what was known as "the ghetto."

German soldiers with tanks

Jewish prisoners forced to clear snow – Poland 1941-2

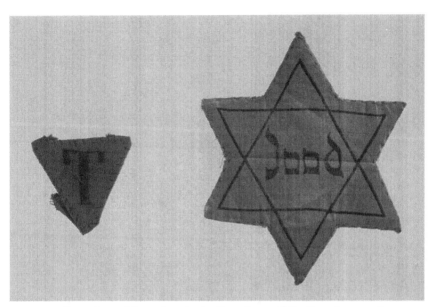

Yellow Star of David with the Dutch word for Jew; Inverted
triangular badge for Tschechen (Czechs)

Jewish teenagers in Poland forced to wear yellow stars

CHAPTER 5

The Nazis' Sadistic Campaign

Before continuing with Abe's story, and in order for it to have the most meaning, it is important to understand the history of the Nazi persecution of the Jews that began in Germany in 1933, long before the start of World War II.

Under the leadership of Adolf Hitler, the Nazis cultivated a nation-wide atmosphere of hatred and intolerance of Jews which only accelerated and intensified each year—until the systematic persecution became outright murder. The Enabling Act of March, 1933, gave Hitler the absolute, unlimited power to carry out his evil plans, which ultimately culminated in "The Final Solution of the Jewish Question"—to murder or expel all European Jews.

From the inception of Hitler's regime, the Third Reich strove to segregate the Jews from the rest of the German population, who they deemed to be of a superior Aryan race. The Nazis accomplished their goal by enacting over 2,000 anti-Jewish measures in Germany which restricted all aspects of Jewish people's public and private lives. The anti-Jewish legislation was enacted in three distinct groups, beginning in 1933. These discriminatory laws against the Jews were publicly announced, reported in the German media, and grew worse each successive year.

Here are some examples of the Third Reich's antisemitic decrees and measures aimed at subverting, and eventually outlawing, the Jewish people:

The first group of anti-Jewish legislation included over four hundred Exclusionary Laws which separated Jews from German society. The first major law was entitled the "Law for the Restoration of the Professional Civil Service of April 7, 1933."[4] It fired most Jews from their civil service jobs, including teachers and professors at public schools and universities, as well as judges and government workers. Later in 1933, Jews were banned from all German sports clubs, associations and facilities. German athletic organizations were now for "Aryans only."

As of October, 1933, Jews were banned from editorial posts.

In April, 1933, Jews could not be admitted to the bar.

In early 1934, Jewish actors were not permitted to appear on stage or screen.

After July, 1934, Jewish law students were no longer permitted to take qualifying exams for a career in law.

As of February, 1935, Jewish students of medicine were no longer permitted to take requisite exams for a career in medicine.

The Army Law of May, 1935, expelled Jewish officers from the army. "Half and quarter" Jews were expelled later.

On September 15, 1935, the Germans enacted a second set of anti-Jewish legislation known as the Nuremberg Laws. The first Nuremberg Law established the swastika as the official emblem of Germany. The second Nuremberg Law stripped the Jews of their German citizenship, deeming them second-class citizens as compared to full citizens of "German or related blood," and denied them the right to vote. The third Nuremburg Law–"The Law for the Protection of German Blood and Honor"—legally defined Jews as a separate race and prohibited them from marrying or having sexual relations with those of German blood. Additional restrictive laws followed.

In December, 1935, a decree prohibited deceased Jewish soldiers from being named among the dead in World War I memorials.

Between 1935 and '36, Jews were banned from public parks, restaurants and swimming pools and their passports were restricted. Jews could not hold public office.

As of January, 1936, Jews were forbidden to serve as tax consultants.

---

4 Many Jews who fought in WWI were exempt from this law until 1935.

Beginning in 1936, the Germans enacted a third round of anti-Jewish legislation which restricted Jews from German economic life. Under this legislation, the Nazis began the process of preventing Jews from earning a living by "Aryanizing" all Jewish businesses, which included removing the Jewish workers and transferring the Jewish businesses to non-Jewish Germans.

As of October, 1936, Jewish teachers were no longer allowed to privately teach "Aryan" students.

Before the August, 1936, Berlin Summer Olympics, Hitler published in the official Nazi paper—the *Völkischer Beobachter*—that Jews and Blacks should not be allowed to participate in the Olympic Games. Hitler only relinquished this position when other nations threatened to boycott the Games. Even so, he would not allow the top Jewish athletes from Germany to compete, but for one token half-Jewish fencer, Helene Mayer. At the Games themselves, the Nazis tried to camouflage their racist regime by temporarily relaxing their antisemitic policies and removing "No Jews Allowed" signs and slogans throughout the city. Unfortunately, the Nazis' exhibition of peace and tolerance at the Games fooled the international community and afterward the Third Reich stepped up its tyrannical reign.

Starting in 1937, Jewish doctors could not call themselves doctor anymore and could no longer treat non-Jews. The licenses of Jewish lawyers were revoked. Passports were no longer issued to Jews.

As of June, 1938, Jews had to register their property and assets, both foreign and domestic. This paved the way for the German expropriation of their wealth.

In July, 1938, all Jewish passports had to be marked with a "Jew stamp" and Jews were issued special identity cards. Soon thereafter, to isolate and segregate Jews further, they were banned from theaters, cinemas, concerts, health spas, beaches, and resorts.

On November 9-10, 1938, *Kristallnacht,* commonly known as the "Night of Broken Glass," was the precursor to the mass annihilation of European Jews. On this night, approximately 1,000 synagogues were set on fire or desecrated, over 7,000 Jewish homes and businesses had their windows smashed and were looted, an estimated 30,000 Jewish boys and men were rounded up, arrested and sent to concentration camps, and about one hundred Jews were killed. Afterwards, Jews were fined and held personally responsible for the damage.

As of November 12, 1938, all Jewish businesses were closed.

On November 14, 1938, Germany enacted regulations making it illegal for Jews to carry firearms or possess weapons.

Starting November 15, 1938, all Jewish children were expelled from public schools. Jews were barred from universities.

In December, 1938, Jewish midwives were banned from the profession.

In January, 1939, it was decreed that Jews with first names of non-Jewish origin had to add "Israel" for males and "Sara" for females. Jewish pharmacists, dentists, and veterinarians lost their approbation.

In 1939, after the beginning of the war, a nighttime Jewish curfew was mandated. Radios of Jewish people were confiscated, and Jews were evicted from their homes without reason or notice. They were forced to live in designated areas of cities called *Judenhäuser*—Jew Houses.

As of February, 1939, Jews were required to turn in their gold, silver, diamonds, and other valuables to the state without compensation.

In 1940, Jewish telephones were confiscated and Jews could no longer receive ration cards for clothes. Jews' use of public transportation was heavily restricted.

In 1941, Jews were forbidden from leaving the country and had to wear the Yellow Star of David marked "Jew" any time they went out in public. Jews could no longer use public telephones and were prohibited from having pets.

In 1942, no Jewish children could attend school. Jews could no longer receive milk or eggs and had to turn in their coats and wool items to the government.

In 1943, it was decreed that Jews had no access to the courts.

From 1943 through the end of World War II in 1945, the Jewish population continued to be deported, shot to death by firing squads, and murdered in mass killing centers. All of their property and possessions were stolen by the Nazis and their compatriots.

Although only a small sampling of antisemitic acts and abuses are depicted in the preceding timeline, these progressively worsening transgressions make it clear that Nazi Germany's persecution and destruction of its Jewish citizenry did not happen overnight. The Jewish people did not wake up one day and suddenly get herded into the gas chambers. The Nazis' anti-Jewish campaign was gradual and pervasive, escalating over the twelve year period from Hitler's appointment to Chancellor of Germany in 1933 until the war's end in 1945.

During Hitler's twelve year reign, the Nazis used extensive anti-Jewish propaganda to indoctrinate both children and adults. The indoctrination of the German youth was of particular focus for Hitler. He targeted young German boys and girls, teaching them Nazi racial principles and antisemitic views so they would become loyal supporters of the Third Reich. By 1935, approximately sixty percent of the young people of Germany had become members of the Hitler Youth.

There was no escaping the Nazis' promotion of Aryans as a master race and the marginalization of the Jewish community. For children, there were sing-a-longs with antisemitic lyrics and Nazi propaganda marches. History was rewritten to advance the Nazi's radical racist views and this "new history" was incorporated into school curricular material. The public burning of books by Jewish authors, or which contained undesirable ideas or viewpoints, was regularly orchestrated.

Nazi ideology appeared everywhere: in antisemitic feature films, newspapers, radio addresses, board games, posters, and children's literature—from pictures books through advanced textbooks. The Nazis were quite overt in their antisemitic campaign which ultimately evolved into their "Final Solution" plan—to eliminate the entire Jewish population.

Adolf Hitler

Hitler salutes the crowd during the Reich Party Day parade
in Nuremburg -1934

Germans saluting Hitler in the rain

A Jewish girl forced to give Hitler a salute for her school photo – 1934

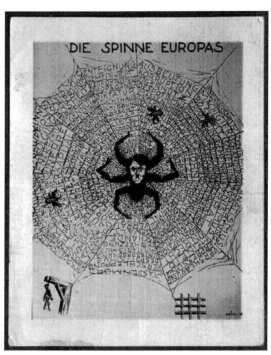

Hitler's web across Europe

Rounding up Jews – Poland 1941-2

A German soldier aims his rifle at five men standing in a row

Posted sign reads 'Jews are not wanted here'

German passport showing Jewish man's forced name change to include middle name Israel

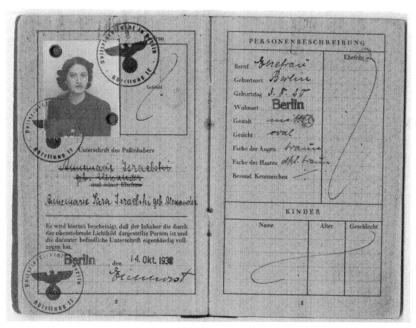

German passport showing Jewish woman's forced name change
to include middle name Sara

German sets two dogs on Jewish forced laborer

Guards confiscate possessions of newly arrived prisoners

Prisoners lined up for roll call

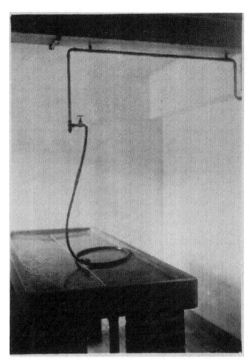

A medical table used for removing gold teeth from prisoners
at the Mauthausen concentration camp

A prisoner who was subjected to low pressure experimentation

Preserved human organs removed from prisoners during medical
experiments conducted in Buchenwald concentration camp

View of a large ditch for mass burias at the Ohrdruf concentration camp

Third U.S. Army discovers looted art treasures hidden by Nazis in a salt mine in Merkers, Germany

Bundles of currency, confiscated art, and other valuables from Berlin are uncovered by U.S. troops in the Merkers salt mine

CHAPTER 6

The Ghetto

A "ghetto" is typically defined as an area of a city lived in by a minority group, especially a run-down and densely populated area inhabited by a group that experiences discrimination. The Nazis, however, created their own variations of "ghetto". They used ghettos to segregate, confine and control the Jewish population of cities and surrounding areas, forcing Jewish people to live in cramped, miserable, dehumanizing conditions.

In Szadek, Poland, in May/June 1940, the Nazis established a ghetto in the worst part of town. According to the United States Holocaust Memorial Museum Encyclopedia of Camps and Ghettos 1933-1945, Volume II, Part A, the Szadek ghetto was situated on two streets encompassing approximately 4,000 square meters. The Nazis evicted Polish occupants from their homes to pack in 110 Jewish families.

Abe has a vivid recollection of the ghetto. "It was small—only a few blocks in area—in the most neglected section … in one of the poorest neighborhoods. They took the Polish out and put us in. The Polish people went to live in our homes—the Jewish homes.

"At first the Szadek ghetto was open, but to make sure none of the Jewish people could freely come and go, the Germans soon enclosed it with a wooden and barbed-wire fence. It was sealed in the summer of 1940. German police were ordered to shoot without warning any Jew who might approach the barbed-wire fence."

Abe lived with his parents, sister and five other families under deplorable conditions, crammed into a small single-family home.

"It was a filthy house. No furniture … just a broken chair. We didn't need furniture. We didn't sit like normal people. We got soup and ate where we were. My father and mother slept in one bed. I slept outside on the floor on a mattress—a bag filled with straw. My sister slept across the room.

"Whatever clothes we had, we wore. New clothes were not available. For washing, we did not have enough soap. For water, there were wells. But there was no bathroom. We had to go outside."

"We were forced to live in overcrowded and dirty conditions. There was no medical care whatsoever. Hygiene was terrible. People had lice."

Before long, scores of otherwise healthy people died from disease and starvation.

Forced Labor in the Ghetto

Abe reports that the Nazis turned the Jewish people of the Szadek ghetto into their own personal slaves. Age and gender were irrelevant; Jewish men, women and children were forced to perform whatever tasks the Germans desired, day or night. When the Germans summoned them, they had to go.

The Nazis forced the Jews to "police" themselves—to do their dirty work for them. By forcing the Jews to create Jewish Councils, the Nazis wanted it to appear as though Jews were in charge so the Jewish people would be more compliant. In Szadek, the Nazis required the Jewish people to form a *Judenrat* (German for "Jewish Committee") and a Jewish police force to ensure German orders were carried out.

"They asked for the tough guys to be the leaders of the Jews, like Kapos [the term for Jewish supervisors in Nazi camps]." The leaders of the Jewish Committee would be in charge of rounding up their own people, who would then be handed over to the Germans to fill their jobs.

"If Germans gave an order to dig a ditch, the heads of the Jewish Committee would come around and say 'I need twenty men.' One of my best friend's father [Chaim Most] thought that he'd save his own life by being a Jewish policeman. But he was murdered too when the ghetto was liquidated."

Although inhabitants of other ghettos may have had shorter work weeks and received some monetary compensation for their labor, Abe recollects that in the Szadek ghetto the Jewish people were forced to work seven days a week without pay. There were no vacations, holidays or sick days for the Jewish prisoners. They could not say "no."

"By 1940, all Jewish men [starting] from fourteen to sixteen years old had to show up at 6:30 a.m. to work. We worked for the Germans doing everything they told us to do.

"I had to go to work doing whatever the Germans wanted. I had to clean barns for horses, work on the railroad. In winter, they sent us on highways to clean roads of snow.

"I remember one incident when it was so bitter cold and I had a pair of gloves, very thin. When I came home after working all day and into the night my mother cooked soup. I held the plate and my mother said, 'Don't hold the plate, it's too hot!' But I couldn't feel it. My fingers were white. To this day, I still have problems with my fingers in the winter."

Abe recalls that women and girls were forced to be slaves for the Germans as well, doing different types of jobs.

"My mother and sister had to go places to work for the SS men. Women cleaned, they were shoemakers, seamstresses. Some of the girls my sister's age would be taken home to officers' houses to help with their families' kids."

Did the Jews in the Szadek ghetto know their fate?

"We'd heard about Hitler since 1933 but did not know about the concentration camps. Before the war, there was one radio in the whole town. We had newspapers—they weren't printed in our town—we got them from Warsaw and Lodz. We had very little knowledge. We heard all kinds of rumors. True rumors like Hitler made a pact with Russia and they were going to build a ghetto in Lodz. We knew this because some people sneaked out and went to other ghettos. At the beginning, some people knew farmers and they sneaked back to bring food."

Did the Jewish people keep their faith while they were being tortured so badly?

"The shul was closed. Jewish people were afraid to get together in a group to pray because the Germans could just come in to kill us. If you showed you were Jewish, you could be shot. But there was praying … most of the time it was in the basement. Someone would be the lookout. If the Germans came, they'd hide everything.. When the Germans came they could do anything they wanted to us—we had no rights."

Starvation

Not only did the Germans chase the Jews into the ghetto, strip them of their valuables, cut off their ability to earn money and force them to perform hard labor, they deprived them of the most basic necessity of life: food.

"All were suffering. Mostly there was very little food in the ghetto. There is hunger constantly. The soup line is the most important time of the day. People are dying from hunger and disease."

The meager food provided by the Germans consisted mostly of soups. In the Szadek ghetto, this "food" was distributed by the Jewish Committee at 4:00 p.m. each day.

"Potato soups, a piece of bread. No coffee. This was the happiest time of the day. We couldn't wait."

But the sparse portions were not nearly enough for the captives in the ghetto who were forced to work long days and weeks. The Jews were treated so appallingly bad in the ghetto that many of them believed things couldn't get any worse. They thought the horrific situation would turn around and get better.

"My grandpa used to say, 'this will not last long.'"

His grandpa's fate? He never made it out of the Szadek ghetto alive.

"He died in our house from starvation. And there was no hygiene, no medicine."

One of Abe's aunts—his father's sister, Lieba Rifka—was only a young woman when she died of hunger in the ghetto as well.

Despite living in a state of terror, under the constant threat of death and subsisting at the starvation level, Abe's mother and father tried to hold their small family together and remain optimistic.

"My parents always gave us hope. 'It will get better, don't cry, don't complain,' they would say. But my sister and I always wanted more food. We were starving."

Escape?

Once the Germans invaded Poland, instituted oppressive laws against the Jews and drove them into ghettos, the danger the Jews faced was undeniable. To escape the Nazi reign of terror, Jewish people abandoned their homes and fled anywhere they thought they might be safer.

"It wasn't hard to get out of the ghetto, but if a German caught a Jew outside he'd shoot him, no questions. To help ourselves was suicide. If you got out, you went to a *Polak* [the Polish word for a Pole] to get a couple of loaves of bread, but you had to give something, like a gold ring."

Polish non-Jewish citizens were strongly encouraged to turn in their Jewish neighbors. "The Germans advertised: If you catch and bring us a Jew who escaped from the ghetto, you'll get paid one pound of sugar."

Just as Poles were rewarded for betraying Jews, hiding Jews meant putting their own lives at risk. "No Poles that I know of helped a Jew. I did hear that Polish people who helped Jews in other towns were killed."

After the German Occupation, food was rationed, so offering sugar as a reward was a major incentive. Abe had heard that a Jewish boy a few years younger than himself was turned in by a Pole in exchange for sugar.

"I could've escaped from the ghetto but I had no place to go. And it was the beginning ... we didn't know they were going to kill all the Jews. We had no weapons."

Abe knows of only one person who successfully escaped from the ghetto.

"One man [named Porteck] ran away from the Szadek ghetto. He married a non-Jewish woman and stayed with her till the end of the war. The woman protected him and after the war he divorced her—they had no kids—and he went to Israel. He married an Israeli and then moved here. His son married a Fair Lawn girl and I went to that wedding.

"A few people came into the Szadek ghetto from other towns when their towns were liquidated. They ran away and came to our town. Some stayed and some went to Lodz. Some of the people who ran away from the small towns went to Lodz because they thought they could survive. There were factories there and they thought they could work for the Germans."

As we now know, there was no safe place to hide or ride out the war in Poland. It didn't matter whether Jews lived in small towns or big cities. If the Nazis found them, they were tortured, and typically killed.

Leaving the Ghetto

One day in the early summer of 1941, after Abe's family had been held in the Szadek ghetto for approximately one year, SS men surrounded the ghetto and ordered that fifty men come with them. Abe was sixteen years old when the Nazis took him, his father, and forty-eight other men away, telling them they were all going to a working camp.

This was the second time during Abe's confinement in the Szadek ghetto that the Nazis had removed a group of fifty Jewish men to perform forced labor. Only one week earlier, they had taken another group of fifty to the Poznan area. "Out of five hundred [Jewish] people, they took out one hundred to the camps."

Although others hid in basements, Abe and his father did not hide because they were told they were going to working camps, which were thought to be good—better conditions than they had in the ghetto. They were promised food and a place to sleep. He and his father also knew that they had no choice but to go with this contingent of fifty men.

"There were no more men that could work. They were either too old or too young, so we had to go with the second transport."

Abe specifically remembers his mom's last words which she shouted as he and his father were being loaded onto a truck to be taken away: "You should take care of the *kinder* [child, in Yiddish]," she yelled to his father. "Abraham, *Zay a mensch!* [Be a decent, honorable person! in Yiddish]," she called to her only son.

Abe never saw his mother again. She and his sister were murdered in the liquidation of the Szadek ghetto.

Liquidation of the Ghetto

On August 14, 1942, the Nazis decided to liquidate the Szadek ghetto—meaning execute all of the Jewish people whom they had forced into the ghetto—then burn it down to the ground to kill any Jews who may have been hiding.

Similar liquidations occurred throughout Europe, where Jews were killed on sight in the ghettos or deported to extermination camps. The Nazis' goal was to make the town *Judenrein*—or clean it of all the Jews.

According to a document Abe recently obtained from the public records archives in Szadek, 404 Jews, including Abe's mother and sister, were murdered in the liquidation of the Szadek ghetto. The Nazis had forced the ghetto occupants into trucks headed for Chelmno, Poland, the first annihilation camp in operation. Chelmno was about an hour's drive away from Szadek, but the trucks were modified so the exhaust pipes pumped toxic fumes into the rear compartment to kill all of the passengers. Only the driver up front was spared. None of the Jewish ghetto inhabitants ever made it alive to Chelmno. Once in Chelmno, the bodies were dumped into a mass grave.

Abe says, "Most were dead. Those who weren't dead they buried anyway."

He now knows that his mother and sister are interred in the mass grave in Chelmno with 365,000 others. Abe ultimately learned the fate of his mother and sister from a non-Jewish Polishman from his hometown who had been a former schoolmate. This man came up to Abe when Abe returned to Poland decades later and recounted the murders. He had personally witnessed the deaths of Abe's family along with those of every other Jewish occupant of the ghetto.

"He saw people fight because they did not want to go in the van. They were shot and thrown in the van."

Sole Ghetto Survivor

Out of the hundreds of Jewish occupants driven into the Szadek ghetto and then liquidated, Abe knows of only one who survived: A woman named Eva Smietanski.

Abe met Eva (called *Chava* in Yiddish) in Kaufering, Germany, after the war and heard her story of narrowly escaping death. It turns out that she had some help from the last person whom one might expect: A Nazi officer's wife.

The irony is not lost on Abe that out of all the people who could have potentially helped to save the Jewish residents of his hometown, the only one who actually did was the enemy. As far as he is aware, none of the non-Jewish citizens of Szadek tried to save any of their Jewish neighbors.

"Only one person in town, a woman who married an SS man, saved a Jewish girl [Eva]."

Apparently, Eva, at sixteen years old, had been a mother's helper for an SS man's wife by day, and returned to the ghetto at night.

"When the SS men surrounded the ghetto and cleaned it all out in one day, the girl wasn't there. She was working in their [the Germans'] home on the day the ghetto was liquidated. The wife told the girl you can't go back because everything is gone. The wife put her in the basement so the husband wouldn't know. She was in the basement three nights until the wife told her husband. When he heard about this he was very upset and afraid for his own life. He couldn't tell or he'd be punished."

This SS man, who was apparently terrified to report that he was harboring a Jewish girl in his home, hid her for the duration of the war—until the Russians liberated the town two years later in 1944. It was through Eva, who was later a guest at Abe's wedding, that he learned how his mother and sister Miriam had fared in the ghetto before they were murdered. Eva is the person who told Abe that his sister Miriam had a boyfriend in the ghetto.

"He [Miriam's boyfriend] was two/three years older than me. I knew the fellow—a nice man. He didn't go to a working camp so he must have been hiding. My best friend Monick Most, his older brother and father—the head of the ghetto Jewish Committee—didn't go either. All were killed when they liquidated the ghetto."

The Szadek ghetto has long since been razed, but Abe possesses one item that evidences his confinement in this miserable enclosure: A black and white photo taken in 1940 which was given to him by another survivor. There are eight men—including Abe—behind a chest-high wooden picket fence with a sign that reads in Polish: "GHETTO, Don't cross or you'll be killed". Beneath the word GHETTO is a large Star of David.

The survivor who gave Abe the Szadek picture was a man a few years older than him named Irving Mendel. Back in Szadek, Abe would see Irving all the time because the *Rebbi* (Hebrew teacher) who taught Abe the Talmud lived in Irving's house. In America, Abe and Irving reconnected when they discovered they lived in the neighboring states of New Jersey and New York, respectively.

Szadek residents forced into a ghetto. Abe is on the far right, his
Aunt Hanna Hinda is second from left

Jewish citizens forced to march with their possessions

Ghetto housing in Poland - 1940

Jewish citizens forced to perform labor

Workers in Lodz ghetto weigh out and distribute food rations

Lodz ghetto children waiting in line in front of soup kitchen

CHAPTER 7

Rawicz

In July 1941, Nazi soldiers rounded up two groups of men from the Szadek ghetto to work in prison camps. The first fifty men were sent to a labor camp near Poznan, a city in west-central Poland, and the next fifty were assigned to work at a labor camp in Rawicz [pronounced *Rah-vich*], a Polish frontier station on the German border. Abe and his father were in the second contingent of fifty, taken together to the same labor camp called an *Arbeitslager*, meaning "working camp."

To get to the Rawicz working camp, Abe and his father were transported from the Szadek ghetto to the train station by truck, then shoved into an airless freight car crammed with dozens of other Jewish prisoners. Although the train trip took a couple of days, they were given no food and barely any water.

Weakened and disoriented, the Jewish men from Szadek alighted from the train to learn that they'd been lied to. Although they'd been promised better living conditions than they'd had in the ghetto, their predicament was now far worse.

"We were told we were going to get three meals a day, we'd get to wash, there would be a place to sleep. Instead, there were a bunch of guys with machine guns around us. What are you going to do?

"The SS men put us up in a six-room house near the river. The house was fenced in with barbed wire. Fifty men slept on the floor in five rooms, the sixth room was the kitchen. We worked twelve hours a day, seven days a week, cleaning the river. They fed us a slice of bread—about four ounces—and black coffee in the morning and watery soup in the evening. I remember being hungry twenty-four hours a day."

Abe estimates the Nazis had twenty camps of fifty to sixty Jewish men at various locations up and down the river. The prisoners were forced to clean the river by immersing themselves waist high into the water, shoveling mud, then tossing it onto the banks. They were given rubber boots with holes.

"We left our shoes on the banks, pulled up our pants and dredged the river. Branches were tied into large bundles with wires and placed along the banks so sand and mud wouldn't wash into the river."

According to Abe, the guards at the Rawicz working camp were extraordinarily brutal, so brutal that they made the guards back at the Szadek ghetto appear tame.

"Things got so bad … every minute … every hour. The watchmen were Ukraine and Polish, not just German. They'd beat us for any little thing. If you said hello to them you got, 'Who are you, my equal?' and if you didn't say hello they'd say, 'Hey Jew, you didn't say hello to me,' and I got smacked. There was no way you could figure out how not to be in trouble. There wasn't a day that I didn't get a smack or hit."

Once an individual was rounded up and sent to one of these working camps, there was no way out, even if his presence in the camp was a mistake. Abe recounts the plight of one man desperately trying to convince the SS men that he didn't belong with the Jewish prisoners, but his pleading fell on deaf ears.

"I knew a guy who died in Rawicz who I'll never forget. He said he wasn't Jewish but he wound up in the camp and died in the camp. This particular man wasn't brought up Jewish but someone in his family—his grandmother or grandfather—was Jewish and they brought him to this camp. He was on a transport from Germany where all the Jews were supposed to be German immigrants or had a Jewish relative. He swore: 'I am not a Jew. I went to church. I'm not Jewish. What do they want from me?' He didn't last long. The last words I heard on his death bed were 'Ich bin kein Jude'… 'I am not Jewish.' He was a little older than me, in his twenties."

As prisoners in the Rawicz working camp, Abe and his father were forced to perform hard labor but were provided with barely enough food to subsist. Even under the most oppressive of conditions, Abe's father still tried to take care of his son.

"My father would give me bread. He told me he got it from somebody. I think he lied and gave me his own bread. My father loved me. At one point in Rawicz he got horsemeat. I don't know how he got it. He wanted me to eat it. I ate it, but then I found out what it was. A guy showed me big bones. I didn't like it, but I was hungry."

Hangings

Abe describes how the starving Jewish prisoners had to walk through sizeable corn fields every day to get from their barbed wire-enclosed house to the muddy river. In the summer, when the full-grown corn was ready to be harvested, anyone caught pocketing husks or kernels was punished with death by hanging.

"Every few weeks, mostly on Sundays, they rounded up all the closest camps to watch. That was our half day off, or we'd go to the hanging after work."

The Nazis used portable gallows to carry out the hangings. After an execution the gallows were transported to the next location. Rather than making the Jewish prisoners mere spectators at theses ghastly events, the Nazis forced them to be active participants.

"There were two steps made of wood leading up to where the person would stand. Jews had to kick away the steps to hang them."

At one hanging Abe was the one asked to kick away the steps. He did not want to, of course, and his reluctance cost him.

"I wasn't fast enough. The guards hollered '*Mach schnell!*' [Hurry up!] and beat me with the butt of a gun. There were a few other people that didn't want to [either]. We were hollered at and kicked. After the hanging everyone was forced to walk around the body."

Abe's Father Dies

Within two to three months, the original fifty men brought in from Szadek had dwindled down to twenty. The living and working conditions were so abysmal that the majority of the men who had arrived at the camp healthy and robust quickly perished. The coldhearted Nazis treated their workers as expendable, simply bringing in replacement crews when the previous sets died.

"Every few weeks new men were sent to our camp to replace the dead. They'd send another transport from Lodz."

Abe refers to the men who arrived from Lodz as the "Jewish Mafioso." He says he uses that name because "they were big, powerful, guys who strong-armed people. They were all the tough guys. They used dirty language—in Yiddish. My father used to say, 'Don't listen to them.'"

Although one might intuitively think these large, hardy, tough men would be the most likely to survive, the exact opposite was true—they were the first to die.

"They died so fast because they were big and strong and needed more food than a smaller, younger man."

As in the Szadek ghetto, there was little to no hygiene at the Rawicz Working Camp. Abe recollects that the Nazis only allowed their overworked, starving prisoners to wash up once a week.

"The washing—we had to wash outside by the river. It didn't matter if there was snow. A lot of people got pneumonia and died. So every couple of weeks new transports of forty to fifty men came. Very strong men, like butchers, became weaklings in days."

Tragically, Abe's father was among the multitude of strong men who did not make it. He died in the spring of 1942, after lasting almost one year in the Rawicz Camp.

"The conditions in the working camp were terrible. Men were dying from hunger and disease. One of the men was my father."

Jacob Pik—whom Abe describes as a very healthy, athletic man before the working camp—contracted typhoid, a life-threatening bacterial disease transmitted through contaminated food or water. At the time of his father's death, Abe had also contracted typhoid and was severely ill.

"I had it, a temperature of 105 degrees. Only very few people didn't get it and they took care of the rest of us."

Abe was deliriously weak when someone woke him one morning to tell him his father had passed. As sick as he was, it is a haunting memory that he will never shake.

"I remember my father was sick. He was laying there with his eyes open. He could hardly breathe. I was very young, I was still strong enough to recover from it but my father died. The older and the very young died."

What happened next still infuriates Abe to this day. Although every atrocity inflicted upon him, his family and all the Jewish people at the hands of the Nazis was incomprehensibly cruel and inhumane, Abe can never get over how he was treated in the wake of his father's death.

He recounts how every morning a buggy came to take away all the dead bodies. Weak and grieving, he asked the *Lagerführer*—the head SS officer commanding the camp—if he could go in the buggy to help bury his father. Instead of granting Abe, a mere sixteen year old child, that small but precious request, the malicious guard slammed the barrel of his rifle into Abe's back and hollered, "You goddamn dog! You go to work!"

In relating this heart-wrenching story, Abe shakes his head and emphatically states, "But there was no work! We were just cleaning up the dead. There were five rooms and you had to go in every hour and take out the bodies. Until today, I don't know where my father is buried. I asked a few people but nobody knew."

Abe believes that the Germans intentionally infected the Jews with typhoid just before they closed Rawicz, then transported whomever was left to concentration camps.

"We knew it. They got the prisoners all together to infect them all ... put barbed wire all around ... there was no contact with the Germans. They closed up all the camps and they did not come in for a couple of weeks. [Before typhoid] they used to bring in the food on horse and buggies. Instead, they pushed in a wagon of food every morning."

Abe's supposition that the prisoners were purposely exposed to the typhoid virus might be true. It is well-documented that in the 1940s, in the Buchenwald concentration camp, the Nazis performed medical experiments with contagious diseases on live prisoners. Although the purported intent of infecting prisoners was to find a cure for the diseases, hundreds of prisoners died from these Nazi experiments with typhoid, typhus, cholera, and diphtheria.

Similarly, most of the prisoners at the Rawicz camp died from the typhoid epidemic. By the time the bacterial disease had run its course, there were only a handful of survivors remaining. Abe—a small, skinny teenager—was one of the few.

"The survivors from the working camp were very young. Most of the older people died. The guards disinfected those who survived with some kind of powder. No medicines were given."

By August of 1943, after Abe had endured two inconceivably horrific years in the Rawicz Working Camp, most of the prisoners were dead and the conditions so deplorable that the camp was closed. The few surviving prisoners were forced into freight cars for a long, arduous journey to the legendary concentration camp in Poland known as Auschwitz-Birkenau.

"We left Rawicz by train—in a cattle car. We didn't know where we were going. We were so packed in, we could only stand. It was horrible there. It was beyond imagination. After twelve hours, people started dying. We pushed them to the side and sat on the bodies. They were so weak and undernourished. It was two or three days with no food, no drinks. At least half the people died."

Weak, frightened, and bewildered, the surviving prisoners did not know where they were when the train finally rumbled to a stop and they were released from the cramped cattle cars. The ominous spectacle before them was one Abe will never forget.

"When we got off the trains it was already dark. There were big lights shining on us. Mengele was there. 'To the left, to the right…'"

Prisoners perform forced labor

CHAPTER 8

Auschwitz-Birkenau

At the infamous Auschwitz-Birkenau death complex in Poland—the largest of the Nazi concentration camps and killing centers—it is estimated that at least 960,000 of the 1.1 million Jews who were deported there were murdered. Hundreds of thousands of Jews were from Poland and Hungary, tens of thousands from Greece, France, Slovakia, the Netherlands, Bohemia, Moravia, and Belgium, and thousands more from Italy, Yugoslavia, Norway, and other countries.

When transports of prisoners pulled into Auschwitz, the new arrivals were finally released from their hellish confinement in overcrowded cattle cars, but stepped onto solid ground to face a new hell. The first thing they saw was uniformed SS men with large guns and fearsome dogs.

Upon Abe's arrival in Auschwitz in August of 1943, he and his fellow captives encountered prisoners in charge, called Kapos. Inmates with the designation of Kapo assisted the SS in supervising other prisoners.

Confused and disoriented, Abe and some other prisoners asked the Kapos, "What's this guy doing? What's going on here?"

They were told by the Kapos: "To the left to the crematoria, to the right to life."

Abe's eyes roll toward the sky as he says, "We saw the chimneys, we saw the smoke. I asked an SS man, 'Where are all these people going?' And he pointed to the chimney. The Kapos would joke, 'You better watch out or you'll be up the chimney!' I didn't know what they meant."

Men and women were permanently separated from each other as soon as they disembarked from the trains. The majority were sent to the gas chambers. Those who were not immediately gassed were deemed fit for forced labor and confined to single-gender camps. Their belongings were confiscated.

"Getting off the train, women and children were told to step forward. Then they went through a 'selection.' They took young women who could work away. All the other women and children were killed."

The Nazis rushed their prisoners along, apparently operating under the theory that if the process moved quickly then it would be easier to murder the victims. "When we got off the train they told us to hurry up, leave your things, we'll get it to you later.

"The men were either given numbers or sent straight to the gas chambers. The majority of the old and the young were taken away to be gassed and the bodies burned in the crematorium. Sometimes men who looked capable of working were saved for a while, even if they were old. It depended how you looked whether you survived … if you were a teenager that looked older and you could work, you didn't immediately go to the gas chamber. The gas chambers and crematorium were working twenty-four hours a day, seven days a week."

Abe depicts the Nazis as cold-blooded killing machines who could not exterminate the Jews fast enough, even if it meant burning them alive. It is incomprehensibly horrific to even think about innocent men, women, and children being burned alive, but there were many witnesses to this atrocious practice and Abe is but one of them.

It may be decades later, but the pain of witnessing the Nazis' burning live human beings is fresh on Abe's face as he recalls what he saw: "When the crematoriums were going at 100% capacity, they made a fire and pushed people in. When a transport of children came, they went right in [to the fire]."

No one was spared. Even those who cooperated with the Nazis and did their dirty work—such as the Kapos—were eventually exterminated. Only certain prisoners who were specially trained on the operation of the gas chambers and ovens (known as the *Sonderkommando*) may have been less expendable than others. However, for the most part, nothing one did for the Nazis was enough to save his life if he was a prisoner, especially a Jew.

Abe witnessed the Nazis' merciless treatment of those who assisted them: "There were people who worked in the crematorium … prisoners. Every few weeks the Germans would take them, gas them, and put new guys in charge of the crematorium."

Although the vicious Nazi guards were not much older than Abe, they were powerful and deadly. Abe describes an extraordinarily cruel, hardhearted class of men who were devoid of humanity, never showing any compassion or kindness.

"SS men were always watching you and they could kill you at any minute for any reason. It's unbelievable but these guys would kill other people for fun. Then they'd say, 'I just killed another Jew' and praise each other: 'You did a good job.'

"The SS men were soldiers … twenty-two, twenty-three, twenty-four years old. Officers were older people. SS men were a special breed. Soldiers had to listen to them. They were Hitler's guard."

Tattoos & Badges

SS Captain Dr. Josef Mengele—the notorious Nazi *Angel of Death*—stood in full uniform, sporting white gloves and a wooden stick, to greet most transports. When the ill-fated men, women, and children were freed from their sealed boxcars, Mengele and other SS officers would look at each prisoner and whimsically point to either the left or the right. If they didn't like the way someone looked, they pointed to the left. Fortunately for Abe, he was directed to the right.

"They called us alphabetically and I was a 'P' and stood off and got a number on my arm. Joe Oputet was right ahead of me. He got one number lower [143449]. A man, one of the prisoners who worked there, told us we were the lucky ones, we got the numbers. 'The other ones are already … look there, at the chimneys.'" Abe aims an index finger skyward as he references the chimneys.

Abe bears permanent evidence of his "good fortune" at being sent to the right. Pointing to numbers that are beneath his sleeve, he says, "We who survived the selection were tattooed on our left arm."

From that moment on Abe was no longer a human being with a name. His sole identity became Nazi Prisoner #143450.

"I was not called by my name, only by my number. In this camp, if you did not have a number, you went to the gas chamber. I had an early number—in this time there had to be at least 500,000 going through Auschwitz-Birkenau. People who came later, after 1943, 1944, didn't get numbers."

The Nazis did not view the Jewish people as fellow human beings, which made it easy for them to completely dehumanize their victims and kill them. Without a name and an individual identity, prisoners were nothing more than lowly, insignificant animals—like branded cattle that could be slaughtered without mercy. By shaving their victims' heads, giving them numbers, forcing them to wear striped prison uniforms, immersing them in filthy conditions, and starving them until they were walking skeletons, the Nazis degraded their prisoners to such an extent that they could be murdered by the guards without a second thought.

Abe reports that each camp prisoner had the same number as his tattoo sewn on the outside of his striped prison jacket—on the front in the upper left. In addition, the Nazis used colored "badges" to distinguish between different categories of prisoners.

"On the lapel of the jacket or overcoat was sewn a yellow triangle for Jews. Gays had pink triangles on their lapels, political prisoners had red triangles."

Jewish prisoners typically had two triangles. A second colored triangle was inverted and superimposed over the first yellow triangle to form the Star of David. For example, a gay Jew would have a pink triangle which pointed downward overlaying his upright yellow triangle.

The Nazis used other badge codes to identify their inmates, such as green triangles for "habitual criminals," purple triangles for "Jehovah's Witnesses," blue triangles for "foreign" forced laborers, red triangles for "political" prisoners and black triangles for those considered "asocial." The asocial classification was used for many types of people whom the Nazis deemed undesirable, such as gypsies, prostitutes, beggars, drug addicts, and the mentally ill. In addition, some camps added color-coded bars over the triangles to denote repeat offenders and a solitary capital letter to depict an inmate's country of origin (e.g., P for Pole). There were even more markings for escape suspects, race defilers, and "special" inmates.

Women & Children

There were approximately 216,000 Jewish youths deported to Auschwitz, but only 6,700 teenagers (3%) were selected for forced labor. Almost all of the others were sent directly to their deaths in the gas chambers.

Abe's thirteen year old first cousin, Ephraim Rappaport (the son of Abe's father's sister—Aunt Mindel) who had been on the train with him from Rawicz, refused to lie about his age. When Abe and Ephraim got off the train in Auschwitz, one of the Kapos had instructed them in Yiddish: "Tell them you're a few years older, otherwise it's no good."

Abe says, "I told him to walk on his tippy toes to look older and say he was fifteen, not thirteen. Behind me was an older man who told him to say he was older … fifteen, eighteen … but he didn't listen. I lost him there."

His younger cousin Ephraim told the truth and was sent to the left, taken away, never to be seen again. Even after all these years, Abe cannot recount this tragic story without breaking into tears.

But Ephraim was not Abe's only relative at Auschwitz who was selected for death. Abe was forced to stand by and watch the annihilation of the remainder of his paternal relatives.

"All of my uncles were taken away. We had three there—two of my father's brothers, one of my father's brother-in-laws. They were all sick, they couldn't walk. Me and a cousin, we never saw them again because they went to the gas chamber and crematorium."

Abe also witnessed the murders of many people he knew from Szadek who were on the same train with him to Auschwitz. "Some of them had been in Rawicz and the other nearby [working] camps. They weren't blood relatives but people from my town."

The Nazis had no use for prisoners who could not work, and immediately disposed of anyone who was too young or ill to perform their forced labor. The Nazis' instant death list included babies, all young children, the elderly, the sick, and the majority of women. As soon as these "unsuitable" prisoners stepped off the cattle car transports in Auschwitz, they were marched straight to the gas chambers. If they were too old or ill to walk, the cars took them directly to Birkenau to be killed.

Besides losing most of his family and being tortured for the majority of his teenage years, Abe laments that he missed having contact with girls for such a long period of time. Back in Szadek he was a typical teenage boy who had girlfriends and enjoyed spending time with his female friends and family. But during the entire length of his internment in the concentration camps, men and women were kept separately. He did not see a female for several more years—until after his liberation in 1945.

"When women were brought in on transports to Auschwitz, they were taken away to a women's camp or sent directly to the gas chamber. Mothers with babies were killed immediately. Only some of the women were allowed to live so they could work at certain jobs, mainly to be slaves for the guards' wives or work in factories. Some were made into prostitutes for the Nazis."

The unlucky women who were selected to be killed after they came off the transports did not immediately know their fate. In order to get them to cooperate, the Nazis lied to them with false promises.

"Some of the Kapos told us that they told the women to hurry up, get undressed, and they'd get a shower. Then, after they were gassed—which took three to four minutes—they had to remove the bodies and put them in the ovens. They had to pull out their gold teeth with a pliers and give them to the Germans."

Abe's lips twist and eyes narrow as he tells of a revolting incident involving a new mother that he personally observed upon his arrival at Auschwitz after departing from the train. "I remember a woman who had a small baby. She wanted to save the baby so she gave the baby something to fall asleep so it wouldn't cry. An SS man saw the woman was holding something big and the SS man stuck a bayonet through the baby. The baby cried. Then she [the woman] was walked away to the gas chambers. That was a normal thing for an SS man to stick a bayonet in a bundle."

Another recollection that haunts Abe to this day is the fate of a transport of young children who had arrived from Belgium or Holland. "The children were all beautifully dressed. There were dozens of them—they were all little—between the ages of five and ten. The trucks dropped them near the crematorium."

He shakes his head and his eyes cloud over as he speaks about the horror he witnessed. "They dropped them off and chased them to the gas chambers. I saw a five year old boy run through a six foot tall SS man's legs and around the building. The SS man grabbed the boy by his legs and smashed his head against the brick wall and he fell down. That SS man probably had children of his own at home. How could he do that to someone else's?"

The unimaginable cruelty of the Nazis did not cease. "Things like that happened every day and we got used to that. It's amazing we survived and didn't commit suicide we saw so much ... that we didn't say we saw enough and couldn't take it anymore. We are very, very strong people."

Another mind-blowingly heinous act against children occurred shortly after Abe's arrival at Auschwitz. He blinks hard and pushes his glasses aside to rub his eyes before describing one of the most gruesome, nightmarish scenes one could ever imagine.

"The first night in Auschwitz, I saw a big fire. Two to three hundred feet away, a pit. They brought a big transport and were burning children. We were in the barracks. We looked out the window. Other people in the barracks told me they burned the children ... with their clothes ... with everything. A religious man started to holler, 'we need to say *Kaddish!*' [the Hebrew prayer for the dead]."

Abe explains, "We needed to say it for ourselves because normally kids say *Kaddish* for their parents after they've died, but now that all the kids were gone, there'd be no one to say it for us. I said it and even those who weren't religious joined in."

Living Conditions

Accommodations in the camps were abysmal. Prisoners were crammed into filthy, overcrowded barracks with no bathrooms. In Auschwitz, Abe was initially quarantined with the other new arrivals for the first couple of weeks. He recalls that he slept in Barrack (also called Block) #15.

"There were maybe twenty, twenty-five barracks. A couple of hundred, maybe a thousand people in one barrack. We used to sleep in three layers—a top, a middle, and a bottom. The whole thing [the bed] was the length of a person. They were all wood, with mattresses filled with straw. We got a blanket to cover us."

Although the prisoners were locked in every evening for a curfew, the Nazi guards entered at will. The prisoners were never safe, not even while they slept.

"SS men would come in in the middle of the night. They'd chase us down and each person would stand in a row. They would smack who they wanted and go out the other side. It was just to wake us up. From eight at night to six in the morning you couldn't get out of the barracks."

Since the prisoners had no access to the outside during the evening hours and the barracks lacked bathrooms, there were frequent "accidents."

"At night you couldn't go out if you needed to relieve yourself [because the doors were locked]. They had a pail on the floor. In the morning you saw the pail wasn't big enough … it was overflowing. People on top who couldn't hold it … things would come down at you. No one wanted to sleep on the bottom."

When the prisoners finally were allowed out of the barracks to relieve themselves, the latrine area they had to use was exceedingly unpleasant. Abe found it to be dirty and disgusting.

"The toilets—called the latrine—were in a long, narrow barrack. There were two rows of seats where you could relieve yourself. First thing in the morning everyone ran toward it. If you didn't get there early you had to wait in line. Some people pushed others off the seats if they couldn't wait. There was no toilet paper. We used to grab big pieces of grass. There were no sinks, no water. There was nothing there. It was terrible."

Without access to water for basic cleanliness, the prisoners had to resort to using rain and snow.

"When it rained people went out and washed themselves a little. When there was snow we went out naked and washed ourselves with snow. It was very cold—a miserable thing—but on the other hand we had water. We'd eat clean snow too."

Birkenau

From the main Auschwitz camp where he'd first arrived, Abe was transferred a few blocks away to neighboring Birkenau, historically known as an extermination camp. Abe refers to Birkenau, the center of annihilation and mass murder at the Auschwitz complex, as "the crematorium."

"I thought I'd get gassed but they took us to get washed. They let us in on one end and they closed the doors, just like [how] the others were gassed, but water came out. We washed ourselves, then they sprayed us with some kind of chemical to delouse us. We left, we got clothing which consisted of a pair of pants, pair of shoes, a shirt, a jacket and a hat. And we went out. This was Birkenau."

Here, he was given his first job: to dispose of the ashes of the poor souls who had been burned in the crematorium.

"They sent us out every morning to spread ashes over large fields. We used to go from the crematorium with wheelbarrows and carry ashes to the fields. The next day we'd get shovels and even the ground. We carried out fifteen foot long rails by hand—similar to [the ones used in] coal mines. A high wagon with four wheels would go on top of it. Then dirt would be brought out to throw over the ashes. We were told they kept bones someplace else. I heard they screened out the bones and buried them."

In Birkenau, similar to Auschwitz, regular "countings" known as *Antreten*—or roll call—were held every morning. Besides accounting for all of their prisoners, the Nazis used the roll calls to weed out those who had withered during the night.

"They were looking for people who were sick—it's called a *selection*. They were taken away."

Selections, similar to those when the prisoners were first transported, occurred on an ongoing basis. Concentration camp prisoners spent every day of their internments knowing that they could be chosen for death at any given moment. Even if they somehow survived extreme starvation, rampant disease, and constant beatings, they were always in danger of being picked out of a lineup for extermination.

Abe recalls that every morning and every night the guards forced the prisoners to stand in lines ten people deep to be counted. They would stand outside, no matter the weather, sometimes for hours. Once every few weeks the Angel of Death, Josef Mengele, would go up and down the lines and randomly point to people. If he pointed to you, you were taken away to be killed. No questions asked.

It seems unfathomable, but Abe relates that sometimes the Nazis murdered large groups of people who were not sick because they had to fill their quotas to kill a certain number of individuals each day. Healthy, able-bodied people were used to fill the gas chambers if there were not enough sick people or new transport victims to keep the crematoria running.

"In the camps we saw them kill the Jews faster. To fill a quota they took capable people who could still work and gassed them. If a train was late, they would take the people who were already in the camp and kill them."

Abe says that he learned about the death quotas from other Jewish prisoners who were assigned to work in the gas chambers and crematoria. "They said they had a quota every day of people they had to kill; otherwise they would be killed themselves. The big chimneys were working day and night with smoke coming out. I saw it."

Abe recounts one instance when a large, unexpected selection occurred. During this random selection, Abe could have easily been one of the people chosen for death, but was somehow spared. Living or dying literally came down to where he was standing amongst a group of fellow prisoners.

"One day when we walked out of the gate, they stopped us and they counted. We were going ten in a row. They counted twenty rows and said, 'You come with us,' and those prisoners turned around and went back. We found out later that on that particular day transports didn't come for some reason and the crematorium and gas chambers had to have their quota so they took any 1,000 people—whatever they needed because the gas chambers and crematorium had to work."

Abe ultimately discovered the fate of the 1,000 people who were at the checkpoint with him in the morning but did not come back at night. He asked around and learned that they had all been murdered.

"I found out later because I didn't know what happened because some of the people were people that I knew. They were all gassed."

At Birkenau, Abe lived in barracks with hundreds of other men from all over Europe. But conditions were so bad in this death camp that prisoners regularly did not make it through the night.

"They were shipped in from their home towns and ghettos. Every morning a couple of people were missing. Kapos would bring out the dead bodies. Everybody would grab something and those bodies would be completely naked."

Fortunately for Abe, he was only in Birkenau a short time, or he might not have made it through the war alive. More prisoners—over 1,000,000—were killed in Birkenau than in any other death camp.

"I was there only a few weeks because I was sent to a coal mine."

Front Exterior view of Auschwitz-Birkenau

View of main camp at Auschwitz

Prisoners disembarking deportation train

Jews awaiting selection on train platform

Mothers and children walking toward gas chamber

Women and children standing on the selection platform at Birkenau

Jewish men having undergone selection are about to be gassed at
Auschwitz-Birkenau

Jewish women and children who have been selected for death at
Auschwitz-Birkenau wait to be taken to the gas chambers

Women and children being led to the gas chambers at Birkenau

Men deemed fit for work after disinfection at Birkenau

Jewish women selected for forced labor march toward
barracks after disinfection and shaving

View of the main camp at Auschwitz surrounded by a barbed wire fence

CHAPTER 9

Jaworzno: Working in a Coal Mine

In the late summer of 1943, after spending several weeks in Auschwitz-Birkenau, Abe was sent to a nearby subcamp (one of more than forty) called Jaworzno [pronounced *Yah-vorshno*]. At this subcamp, which he estimates was approximately ten to fifteen miles from Auschwitz, he was forced to work as a slave in a coal mine known as *Rudolphsgrube* (Rudolph's Mine).

Upon his arrival at Jaworzno, Abe relied on his instincts to help him survive. With no family or friends to lean on or guide him, he needed to stay alert and think on his feet. The first thing he did was to volunteer for masonry work, even though he had no previous experience in this field.

"When I came to Jaworzno they were building a brick fence around the camp—they were looking for masons. I raised my hand, said I was a brick layer. I *schlepped* [carried] bricks. Then, when the fence was finished, they sent me down to the coal mine. In the mine, they wanted ninety-five percent of us to shovel coal. We loaded train wagons with the coal. People were dying like flies. If they saw someone couldn't work anymore, they killed them and threw their body on the wagon."

Since it was clear to Abe that if he kept shoveling coal it would destine him to certain death, he knew he had to get transferred to something less treacherous. As soon as the opportunity presented itself, he volunteered to work as a mason again.

"As we came down into the mine one day they asked who is a mason? I raised my hand again. I said I was a mason. The SS man called me dirty words. He looked at me and said '*You're* a mason?' He told me I was too young …

I couldn't be a mason. I was seventeen then but I told him I was a couple of years older. But he took me anyway because no one else volunteered."

Abe's luck continued when he was assigned to assist a Polish miner/mason who was a regular citizen, not an inmate. This man shielded him from the savage Nazi guards and occasionally snuck him some food.

"There was a Polishman, a really experienced miner. I worked with him. I was his helper. I got lucky, I got a foreman which was a civilian Pole. He was not a prisoner. He lived in and went home at night. He let me rest, once in a while he'd give me a piece of bread. When he saw the Germans coming he'd tell me to do certain things because he was afraid of them too."

At times their relationship was mutually beneficial. Abe didn't have very much, but he gave this man whatever he could to stay in his good graces.

"He liked me. He told me where to hide. When I left Birkenau, they [the Nazis] gave us new clothes. They'd throw them at us and I got two shirts. I gave one to this man. I cut the tops of my high [leather] boots and gave them to him. He went to the shoemaker and had boots made from that leather. There was very little during the war."

Abe explains how he and the Polish miner accomplished the masonry tasks required by the Nazis. Essentially, he and the miner would build arched wooden frames and fill them with bricks to support the ceilings down in the coal mine.

"The Germans were beating the walls to see if they were hollow. They were afraid they'd fall down. We had to build brick enforcements that stopped the ceiling from falling down. It was a round-curved ceiling, like an igloo—a wood structure with pillars. We cemented bricks in. A day later we took the wood [frame] down."

The Horrors of the Coal Mine

What seventeen year-old wants to work in a dark, dirty coal mine? Naturally, Abe was terrified, but as a prisoner he did not have an option.

"Sure I was scared, but what choice did I have? I had to do it. To say no means I have a death sentence."

Every aspect of working in the coal mine was hazardous, starting with the means of descending below ground. Abe did not have the benefit of modern high-speed elevators outfitted with safety features like we have today. He and his fellow prisoners were dropped into the dismal, dark mines by primitive machines with no doors, sensors or safeguards.

"A metal box on a heavy metal rope lowered us down. There were one hundred people going down. Five to six boxes took three to four minutes to go down a couple of hundred feet. It had a motor to get us up."

Deep in the coal mine, the prisoners were guarded by SS men with machine guns as well as German miners. The ruthless guards regularly murdered their captives. Despite being grossly overworked, and continuously underfed, the severely weakened laborers were still expected to perform their strenuous tasks at top speed. Abe grimaces, swinging his head back and forth in disgust as he says, "They killed people if they weren't shoveling fast enough."

To truly understand the degree of horror and misery Abe faced each day in the coal mine, one need no look no further than the inordinately high death toll of his fellow slave laborers. Since the Nazis placed absolutely no value on the lives of these "expendable" prisoners, they habitually killed them, then brought in more.

With inadequate clothing, scarce food, minimal rest and ruthless guards hovering every moment, it is incredible that Abe survived this portion of his imprisonment. But somehow, he made it through two years of mining hell.

"The conditions were terrible. Our clothing consisted of a shirt, pants, jacket, shoes, and a hat. No underwear. They gave us a slice of bread—3 to 4 ounces—black coffee and soup. People were dying faster than they could be buried. Replacements were coming daily."

It did not help that the barracks were not close to the coal mine. Abe and his fellow prisoners were forced to travel by foot to their work site for each shift, irrespective of the weather. Abe's wrists were shackled by iron chains to five to ten other prisoners, who, tethered together, had to trek two miles each way between the barracks and the coal mine.

This walk to work was exceedingly arduous for many reasons. Besides being extremely weak, starved, underdressed, chained to other human beings, and guarded by brutal soldiers with machine guns, Abe and the other slave laborers had to endure the unabashed animosity of local citizens who routinely hurled insults and racial epithets as they went by.

"We passed signs to Krakow walking to work. When we went through the town we heard the slogans, 'Dirty Jews, Christ Killer Jews, Damn Dog Jews.'"

The Night Shift

Working in the mines was dark, dirty, and dangerous—certainly not a place for a teenager. But in his efforts to withstand the wretched situation and survive, Abe volunteered for the one shift which was not supposed to be as bad as the others: the night shift. For two inconceivably grueling years, when almost everyone else went to sleep, Abe set out on the night shift to *Rudolphsgrube*.

"I was told there were three shifts—day, afternoon, and night. If I could get into the night shift in the coal mine, it's the best shift because there's not so many supervision. We worked eight hour shifts but it took an hour just to get there and an hour to get home. We were black from the coal mine. They gave us cold water just to wash our face. Cold water even in the winter. We wore the same dirty clothes every day."

Down in the coal mines the Nazis did not allow the prisoners to handle dynamite. Instead, they brought in experienced outsiders.

"Sometimes we worked with non-prisoners. Like in the mines. They would use civilians—*shteigers*—to handle the explosives."

The prisoners would drill into the rock to bore the holes, then stay back while the civilian *shteigers* stuffed the holes with dynamite and set off the explosives.

"The dynamite—a round stick—they stick it in the hole. It has ten to fifteen long strings [wicks]. Then he lights it and runs away."

Even though the *shteigers* were mostly German civilians, not Nazi soldiers, they were just as deadly. If a *shteiger* directed a German guard to shoot people because they weren't working hard enough, the guard would execute them immediately. Abe relates that the Jewish prisoners were under constant attack by the *shteigers*.

"In the middle of the night a *shteiger*—an engineer in charge, or German foreman—used to come. The *shteigers* were mad. They killed people left and right … at least one a day … sometimes five a day. They had canes with metal hammers at the top that they used to test the walls and ceiling of the mine shaft—to see if they were hollow. The *shteiger* was a son-of-a-bitch—he killed plenty of Jews. If the German caught you sleeping, he'd hit you over the head with the metal hammer and kill you. If you didn't work fast enough, he'd kill you. Then they'd have us throw the body on the *lore* wagon [on top of the coal] that was pushed by the prisoners to ship up [in the elevator]."

The section of the mine Abe worked in was known as the *Wasserschacht*—German for "water pit." He would spend most of his time underground, standing ankle-deep in water while getting dripped on.

"We were very deep—about two hundred feet below ground. It was always wet. Water always dripped down. We would usually work in water up to our ankles. They had pumps to take it out but they didn't care about us. The rubber boots we got had holes. The Poles and Germans didn't wear them anymore so they gave them to us. We were always wet. We had an overcoat with rubber … also second hand [like the boots] with holes. Many, many of my acquaintances that I knew got killed and couldn't survive it."

Miraculously, Abe endured two hellish years of these intolerable conditions during his enslavement in Jaworzno. He credits the Polish foreman he worked with for his survival.

"I was in the coal mine to January 1945. I would have died if it wouldn't be for that man ..."

SS officers outside coal mine

Lore wagon

CHAPTER 10

Jaworzno: Daily Life

Food

Occasionally, the prisoners would be the recipients of small acts of kindness from the civilians who worked in the mines. Even a tiny scrap of bread could make a huge difference in a starving person's survival.

Abe greatly appreciated any gift of food, no matter the size. He didn't receive handouts very often, but, as a famished teenager, every morsel of food helped.

"In the coal mine, once in a while, an experienced *Polak* miner would give me a piece of bread. Sometimes the civilians would give the prisoners cigarettes, which they would trade between one another."

Abe shakes his head in amazement when he recounts the unsettling story of those prisoners—including his friend's father—who gave up food for cigarettes, and then died. He literally watched starving human beings trade their lives for cigarettes.

"It's unbelievable. People gave away food for cigarettes." Although he admits that he doesn't understand this bizarre behavior, he surmises, "maybe it's because with the cigarettes they didn't feel the hunger."

Then he tells another tale about French Jews who were brought to the camps. To survive, they ate animals that Abe found too unsavory to try.

"The French Jewish people in the camps ate frogs. They hit them against the shovel to kill them. When they'd get soup, they'd throw the frogs in the soup. If they were still alive, they'd kill them."

Abe concedes that he could not bring himself to eat the frogs, as hungry as he was. He also describes how he was still selective when he got ahold of a potato in the camp. Even starving, he did not care for the gritty texture of dirty potato skin and would meticulously remove it.

"I was very picky. When I got a potato I would peel it. There were guys that would take my peels and eat them, but they weren't washed.

"Soup came in a big vat. A survivor ladled it. No one wanted to be the first to take it because from the top it's water. If the guy who served knew you, he'd give it to you from the bottom. Or, if you were last in line, you'd get the thicker soup from the bottom.

"In the morning we got a slice of bread—three ounces. At night we got soup. If you complained or asked for thicker soup you got hit with something. The Kapo would hit you with a stick he always carried."

Kapos

The Kapos were prisoners who the Nazis recruited to keep the other inmates in line. Not wanting to die, many of the prisoners who served as Kapos thought that if they took on this important but unpopular role, then they would increase their own chances of survival.

"Some Kapos would hit you to show the Germans they were doing their jobs. They thought that by going along with the Nazis they'd survive. Then what happened? SS men would come along and put those Kapos right into the crematorium and new Kapos would come in.

"Some Kapos were human. There was one, my landsman—Felix Shmetanski—who couldn't hurt a fly, but he hollered whenever he saw an SS man. He'd yell, 'Do this, do that.' But once an SS man saw he wasn't doing his job hurting anyone, he beat him up. After liberation, I was with a Kapo who survived who told us he was Kapo about one month. He did what the Germans told him to do to survive."

Did any of the Nazis ever show any compassion to their prisoners?

Abe immediately dismisses this question with a quick, sharp, "No!"

Survival

Abe had no illusions about his fate at the hands of the Nazis. He saw how swiftly and effortlessly the Nazis took the lives of those around him and understood that, in the eyes of his captors, his life was meaningless.

Survival was highly unlikely in an environment where Jews were so deeply despised that there was no civility or humanity in the way they were treated. Abe relates that the status of a Jewish prisoner was less than that of a dog from the standpoint of the Nazis.

"You couldn't win talking to SS men. If you didn't take off your hat you got hit. Next time, you take off your hat, and they hit you because you took it off. They'd say, 'Are you my friend? My equal? You should've saluted me!'"

The prisoners were so far "beneath" the SS guards that they never addressed any of them by name. If they wanted to get someone's attention they'd yell, "Hey you!" or "You fucking Jew!" Otherwise, the prisoners were called "Goddamn dogs" or referred to by the numbers sewn on the outside of their jackets, which matched the numbers tattooed on their forearms.

"We knew they were out to kill us. The question was what to do to survive. We were very alert to what was going to be. Survival was our goal. It wasn't like here, people worry about getting more money."

Survival in the camps essentially came down to getting more food. The prisoners were subsisting at starvation levels, and Abe, in particular, knew that he could only last for so long. Too many around him had perished from prolonged starvation.

"The main thing on my mind was to get a piece of bread, to get some food. We thought about surviving, but we didn't have a lot of hope for it. We were fighting to live when we were hungry—we wanted to survive. It's just a matter of time when you give up the fight to live.

"Every human being wants to survive and I was no different. I met some good people, they liked me, they knew my parents, but they were as hungry as I was ... they couldn't help me. We were all like brothers—we suffered the same thing. We all got beat up for nothing, we got very little to eat."

There were other compelling reasons why Abe and his fellow prisoners wanted to survive. Perhaps the primary one, which many survivors seem to share, was to tell the world about what was done to them.

"We wanted to survive so we could tell people what's happened. There's tradition, *Kaddish* [prayer for the dead], *Yahrzeit* [anniversary of the death of a loved one]. We needed to be alive to say *Kaddish* for all those people killed. I felt my family, my loved ones, deserved that—that someone should be around to talk about it. If I'm the only one left and I was killed, who else would do it?"

But time was not Abe's friend. The more years that passed, the more Abe's chances of survival diminished. He became weaker and feebler every day in captivity.

"With every year that went by we saw it clearer. The religious Jews thought this can't go on, they won't kill us. Then they hanged us, shot us, starved us. First, I started losing weight. I was turning into a *Muselmann* [German term for a prisoner who was near death]. I was always hungry. I saw all the people dying around me. I had the will to live but not the means or the strength."

Keeping The Faith

Abe relates how some Jewish prisoners still clung to their faith and tried to observe the Jewish holidays in spite of the living hell in which they had been immersed.

"The very religious knew the Jewish calendar and would lead prayers in the barracks. We'd come back and be tired and dirty and hungry and one guy would say, 'It's Rosh Hashana.' He remembered all the prayers for Yom Kippur. We didn't have books, *talits* [prayer shawls] or anything. We just had ourselves."

How did Abe handle a holiday such as Passover which requires that one *not* eat bread for eight days?

"On Passover we'd eat the bread because it says in the Torah that to save a life you can break all the laws. I didn't think about it. There were others who thought about it."

Besides the differences in how the religious and not-so-religious prisoners kept their faith during their internment, there was also a large disparity in viewpoints between the older and younger prisoners. From Abe's portrayal, the older folks seemed to retain their optimism while the younger ones faced the grim reality head on.

"We used to get together … young people, a few boys. We'd sit down, every second Sunday afternoon. We talked about what we were going to do if we survived. I said, 'I'm going to eat till I bust!' Another said, 'I want the Germans to feel what we feel.' And another, 'I'm going to wash every day.' We were dreaming. In real life, the way we were watched and treated, we knew we had a death sentence. They were going to kill us–shoot us, beat us to death, starve us. We knew the longer it takes [to be freed], it's a matter of time, or we won't make it.

"We were all young kids. The elders had different opinions. We walked away from their discussions. They were saying we had to be good, they're not going to kill us all. We were too young to argue with them. They had a lot of faith in God and other things. We'd say, 'Where is God? While we're being slaughtered down here, God must be on vacation. Why us? What did we do to deserve this kind of thing? What did babies do? Why did God let children be killed?' Until today I have more questions than answers from God."

After personally witnessing the mass murder and torture of tens of thousands of innocent people, Abe and his fellow inmates were furious that no one else tried to stop the atrocities. They couldn't imagine that other civilized nations approved of the Nazis' annihilation of the Jewish people.

"In the camps we were arguing, discussing things. We were blaming the world. We didn't know America so well. Other neighbors—Russia, France, England—didn't come to help us. How come? I was in Auschwitz when they took away thousands to feed the gas chambers. We were saying, 'Why didn't they come bomb the railroads?'"

Abe had been held captive by the Nazis for almost five years before he first heard the sounds of war, which to him, meant his rescuers were closing in. The real question, though, was whether he could hang on that long.

"In the beginning of 1945, we'd lie on the ground and hear explosions far away … when the Russians were going west. So even then we knew it would end, but when? Will I survive? Will I have the strength? Will I get shot for no reason at all? We'd already given in to hunger … that we didn't have clothes for winter. We were freezing. Will it come to an end, and when?"

Abe's Guardian Angel

If there is such a thing as a guardian angel, then Abe Peck has one. He had two near-death experiences in Jaworzno from which he never would have made it out alive but for his guardian angel who appeared in the form of a man named Shama.

As a small boy, Abe could never have known that the young neighborhood girl from Szadek who worked as his mother's helper was going to marry the man who would save his life. During his early childhood years, Abe had been cared for by Shama's wife, Hannah Nacha, who was nine or ten years older than Abe. He remembers that Hannah Nacha used to tote him around when he was little.

"When I was ten to twelve she was in her twenties. She married a guy [Shama] from another town who I knew. I met this guy in Jaworzno … in the coal mine. He recognized me. I said Hannah Nacha was my babysitter– she carried me. One day we were told we'd work in the Water Shaft [in the mine]. I didn't know I should carry my boots and put them on there. I tried to put them on and got kicked in the ass by the Kapo and fell face forward in the mud. This guy Shama stopped the Kapo from beating me. He was in the mafia. He sold stolen goods. He saved my life."

Abe further explains his reference to the mafia: "In Poland, every city had strong men—like the mafia today. Polish business owners would pay these men to protect their stores."

A few days after the Water Shaft incident, Abe's guardian angel, Shama, intervened on his behalf yet again. This time, it was to save him from the Angel of Death, Josef Mengele.

"He [Shama] was in the same barrack as me. I was on the night shift from 6:00 p.m. to 6:00 a.m. The hours of the shift were different depending on the SS man in charge, but we always worked eight hours. Every month Mengele would come to Jaworzno and look for selection—who couldn't work—and take them to the crematorium. I was put in a group to go to the crematorium and fifteen minutes before I was going to be taken away, this man Shama, who was a foreman, told Mengele in German, 'What did you take that man for? He's a good worker.' Mengele responded that I'm a *Muselmann*. We were standing behind a table, all ready to go to the gas chamber."

Abe's guardian angel, Shama, took off his hat and bowed humbly before the Angel of Death. "No, he's very good," he told Mengele, "one of my best workers." Abe was then removed from the sickly group slated for death and returned to the assembly of workers headed out to the coal mine.

Does Abe know what made Mengele think he was a *Muselmann*?

"Yes," he explains, "You know someone is *Musel*—dying—because you see it every day. This was a common, common thing."

What ultimately happened to Shama?

Shama survived the camps too, but the rest of his life took on a sorrowful twist. After the war he did not know that his wife Hannah was still alive, and he married another woman in Italy, where he'd moved after the war.

Dogs

Despite how inhumanely the German guards treated the concentration camp prisoners, Abe will be the first to tell you that they really liked and took great care of their dogs. During his imprisonment, Abe saw that thousands of human inmates were dying of starvation, but the Nazis' canine contingent was well-fed.

"They used German Shepherds to keep the prisoners in line. The Germans fed the dogs better than they fed the prisoners. The dogs were regularly given soup and meats. The dogs were kept chained up by the barbed wire fence. Me and two other boys decided to get our stomachs filled up so we'd steal food from the dogs. The way we'd do it was plain ingenuity. We got sticks, inserted curved nails on the ends, and pulled pots of the dogs' food over for ourselves. We threw stones at the other end of the dogs' chains and the dogs would run for the stones and we pulled the dogs' bowls."

In Jaworzno, Abe and the other boys were only able to steal food from the dogs two or three times. They were too fearful of the consequences to continue.

"I think they caught someone and hanged them, so we had to give it up. If we were caught, it would've been certain death. We were afraid the dogs were going to get us or a bullet would get us. To kill a dog was terrible for a German, but to kill a person was nothing."

He emphasizes that "life was very cheap—you could be shot or hanged [for anything]. I wouldn't do it [take the chance] today."

One of the other two boys who had stolen the dogs' food with Abe also survived the camps. "I met him after the war."

Acknowledging that stealing food from dogs sounds farfetched, Abe adds: "It looks like made up stories, but it's true."

Hygiene

During the entire time Abe was held prisoner by the Nazis, he was never given any soap, shampoo, combs, toothbrushes, or toothpaste. He and the other prisoners were perpetually filthy.

"You rubbed your gums with your finger. You took off your shoes and overcoat and slept in your clothes. There was no washing. I rubbed my feet with sand to clean them."

In Jaworzno, the inmates were only allowed to wash their faces upon their return from the coal mine once each day, even though they were always covered from head to toe in black soot. They were given showers once every two weeks, but the showers were outside.

"Every second Sunday, we were ordered to strip out of our clothes, leave them in the barrack and run naked across the camp to the showers. We ran in the rain, the snow, the cold."

When the prisoners reached the showers, they were sprayed with water that only varied between cold and lukewarm. Never hot. There were no towels to dry off. Drenched and freezing, they had to run back across the camp to retrieve their prison clothes. Many got pneumonia.

Abe says, "How I survived? Don't ask me. I don't know."

Dog wearing swastika used by SS

Hair Care

There were no barbershops or salons in concentration camps. During Abe's captivity, the Nazis simply stripped their prisoners of all hair.

"Every few weeks we got a haircut. A haircut consists of not just cutting the hair from the head. It was the whole body. Can you imagine standing there, naked, bending over, getting shaved? They did the same thing to women. They told us it was for hygiene. I was talking to Helen [Abe's wife] and she said the same thing. They did not have any hair. They [the Nazis] used a machine—like an electric razor but by hand. Sometimes they would cut your skin. There was nobody there that cared about you if you were bleeding. If you die, you die."

Lice were a pervasive problem in the camps. The prisoners were forced to submit to constant *Entlausung* [delousing] through sprays, powders, and shaving.

"We were shaved everywhere … we had no hair, but nothing got rid of the lice. We mostly worked seven days a week. Every second Sunday we got off for the *Entlausung*."

Foot Care

There were no scissors or appliances for cuticle care. Abe had to improvise to try to take care of his nails.

"If we got a piece of metal—from the top of a can—we tried to sharpen it on two stones and then tried it on our feet to cut our toenails. When we came out of the camps our nails were growing back into our flesh."

As for footwear, the prisoners used the shoes of others who had been murdered in the camps.

"Sometimes they [the Nazis] gave us wooden shoes … if the people that were killed were Dutch. You picked shoes from a stack … found your size … they were from the dead prisoners."

"In 1944 we heard rumors—the Germans talked and were over-heard by prisoners. Russia stopped them at Stalingrad and was pushing them back. This was the Eastern front. We also heard the Americans were coming. Someone said they saw an American plane over Auschwitz. A few months later if you laid on the ground you could hear artillery fired. It was true."

Miraculously, despite the extraordinarily punishing conditions, Abe survived two years of servitude toiling in the coal mine, until January, 1945, when the Nazis forced the prisoners out of the camp and onto one of the infamous Death Marches.

CHAPTER 11

Death Marches

Abe recounts that in January, 1945, when the Allied troops drew closer, the German guards started to run, emptying out the concentration camps. Instead of abandoning their prisoners, the SS men forced them at gunpoint to leave the Jaworzno and Auschwitz camps.

On January 17, 1945, two days after Jaworzno had been bombed by Russian planes, tens of thousands of prisoners headed out of the camps and into the icy cold wilderness, embarking on one of the infamous Death Marches.

"They didn't know what to do with us ... they still pushed us around. One night they told us tomorrow morning we're moving out. So they took us on the Death March."

No one informed Abe and the other prisoners why they were fleeing the camps, but they intuitively knew.

"We were leaving because of one reason: The Russians were moving closer and they had to evacuate. They got the whole camp out on the Death March. We marched for days."

Since the camps were segregated, there were no women on this march.

"All strictly men from Auschwitz and Jaworzno."

As they trudged through the woods, across the snow, over the mountains, they were joined by occupants of smaller concentration camps which they passed along the way. Until this Death March, Abe had been confined with predominantly Jewish prisoners in the camps. Once they were on the run mixing with other prisoners from these smaller camps, Abe discovered he was in the company of English prisoners of war.

"It was so bad. We walked for several days in the freezing cold with no food or water. A lot of people said they had enough, they couldn't take it. They didn't want to survive. Thousands fell down. Many people froze to death or got shot because they couldn't walk any more. Thousands froze. From over 20,000, only 1,500 survived that march."

It is truly miraculous that Abe did survive the Death March from the Auschwitz camp system considering that the vast majority of prisoners—tens of thousands—perished under the brutally harsh conditions. The odds were far greater that Abe would have succumbed to starvation, sickness, exposure, exhaustion or have been murdered like the bulk of the others.

Although Abe was unspeakably tired, cold, and hungry, as well as suffering from painful frozen feet, he still had the spirit to live. In spite of his extreme misery, he marched on, through the deep snow.

"We took shoes from the dead people on the side when our feet were wet and cold. To stay hydrated, we ate snow during the Death March, but it made me sick—gave me diarrhea. So I ran all the way to the front of the line to relieve myself since the SS men stayed in the back with machine guns to kill whoever was slow. If you left the line they shot you. I took too long to get back in line and the SS men fired at me."

Inexplicably, none of the bullets from the burst of machine gun fire hit Abe, but he saw them in the snow in a circle all around him. The dark bullets literally outlined the spot where he'd stood.

"I'm a strong believer in luck," he says. "If you've got years [left to live], not even a bullet can kill you."

It was an incredibly sad, sobering realization for a young boy, but Abe knew that if he was hit by the bullets, it would not have mattered to anyone. He was truly on his own.

"When I got shot at, nobody knew who I was. No one would've cared if I was dead."

Indeed, there were miles of frozen corpses in the wake of the March. If Abe was not able to quickly adapt to his new surroundings in the wilderness, he would have undoubtedly perished too.

"Most of the time we were outside in snow. I learned if you keep the snow all around you, you can stay warm. At night we had nowhere to sleep so we slept in the snow or in farmers' barns. Some people tried to hide themselves behind straw so they wouldn't have to return to the March but the Germans got smart and punched the hay with bayonets."

As if the dire predicament of their prisoners wasn't pitiful enough—with most on the brink of death—the Nazis would torture them further for their own amusement. Abe gives an illustration of the Nazi's sadistic tendencies:

"On the Death March if SS men wanted to have some fun, they'd grab a prisoner's hat and throw it into the snow. It was freezing–below zero–so when the prisoner went to get the hat, he'd step out of the line and the SS men would shoot him."

Without exception, the Nazis were extraordinarily heartless and cruel, but there was an interesting change in attitude among fellow prisoners that Abe detected as the war was nearing an end. While on the Death March, he noticed a difference in the way he was treated by non-Jews.

"There were some groups of non-Jewish prisoners, like Russians and Polish prisoners. During the war the Russians and Poles were friends of the Germans, but when they were losing, they'd help [the Jews]. Now that the war was coming to an end, on the March, when SS men didn't see, the Poles and Russians would give the Jews some bread."

As the seemingly never-ending Marches continued, with the majority of prisoners dying around him, Abe needed to find a way to survive. He drew on the power of his own thoughts to pull himself through.

"We were thinking, 'What are we going to do when we make it? I'm going to marry a rich girl,' all crazy things. We weren't just thinking [about surviving] … we tried. Like on the Death March, the will that we want to live carried us."

Abe sums up his survival in only a few words: "I was lucky and sharp. To make sure I didn't get shot. I was lucky every day. They could do at any time what they wanted. Everyone in the camps, we all had a death sentence. I didn't want to give up. The minute people gave up…"

Bodies of prisoners who perished during the evacuation of Auschwitz-Birkenau. Those who fell were killed on the spot- January 1945

Long line of prisoners on Death March

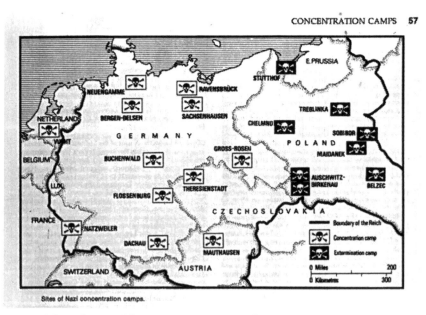

Sites of Nazi concentration camps.

Map of major Nazi concentration and extermination camps

CHAPTER 12

Blechhammer

As the Soviet armies from the East swept closer, Abe heard their artillery through the ground and saw the orange glow from their weapons illuminate the night sky. Knowing that the enemy was closing in, the Nazis forced their prisoners to march to Blechhammer, another of the Auschwitz subcamps.

Once in Blechhammer, Abe and the other starving, exhausted inmates who had managed to survive the grueling Death March out of Auschwitz/Jaworzno and other camps, were quickly relocated. On approximately January 21, 1945, with no opportunity to recuperate, the prisoners were crammed into freight cars on a train bound for Buchenwald—one of the largest Nazi concentration camps, situated in east-central Germany.

"We stayed in Blechhammer one day, then we were put on a train, packed in like sardines. We were standing up, breathing on each other. They were pushing in more, getting in as many as they could, then they closed the doors. Everything was so tight. We couldn't even sit down, but after a few hours some of the people collapsed."

The grisly train trip to Germany took several days. Similar to Abe's initial transport to Auschwitz, the conditions on board were appallingly inhumane. The weak and emaciated passengers, fresh off the debilitating Death March, now died from extreme thirst and hunger. The Nazis gave them no provisions and did not even open the doors.

"We didn't have where to relieve ourselves. Before you know it, there were dead bodies, people falling down." Without any place to put them, the surviving prisoners ended up pushing the corpses against the walls of the box car and sat on the bodies.

After days of suffering, the nightmarish journey came to an abrupt halt when Abe's train came under attack by the Allied forces. Parked at a refueling station, the train was hit by fire from Allied fighter planes.

"They [the Nazis] used old fashioned locomotives. They had to stop to fill up the coal and the water. While the train was at a station it was bombed by the Allies—they didn't know there were prisoners on there. They saw SS men walking … they took us for a military train. Bombers dropped bombs on the tracks. They came very low with machine guns shooting through the [train] cars. We all fell on the floor. I was on the bottom. There were people on top of me."

Within moments of the Allied air assault, the German soldiers fled and the prisoners jumped off the train. The prisoners did not know exactly what was happening, but for the moment they were free.

"We saw uniforms, then guards. There was shooting … someone opened the train and we all ran out. The guards ran away to a bunker. I threw bodies off myself but when I stood up I was full of blood. I said, 'That's it. I'm hit!' But it was from other guys on top of me.

"The first thing we did was run over to a steam locomotive which had a water tank—used to make the steam. We'd been on the train two or three days and needed food and water. They didn't feed us like normal people. I hadn't had a drink in days … people were dying like flies. Bullets had made holes in the tank and warm water was coming out the holes. We drank that water first. Then I smelled food.

"Survivors make fast decisions. We had to decide between life and death. When I came off the train I smelled the food and made a decision really fast to run up the stairs of the railroad station house. Dinner was cooking on the stove. I turned the whole pot over on the table, the soup ran down and I grabbed a piece of meat and put it in my pocket. I turned around and saw blood on the floor. My big toe got hit by shrapnel. I saw it and started to limp. I went back outside and sat on the tracks under the train to eat the meat. I peed on the wound and ripped off a piece of my shirt to tie around it."

During the brief time period when Abe had raced into the railroad station house to get his meat, some of the other prisoners had run to a nearby store a couple of blocks away and grabbed sugar off the shelves. Once the prisoners were back on the train, Abe saw the sugar and asked for some but no one would share.

"They came back with boxes. It looked like sugar. It was sweet like sugar. I begged them to give me a piece but they wouldn't give me any."

As fate would have it, if Abe had eaten the sugar, he probably would not have survived the trip from Blechhammer. It turned out that the white grainy cubes were not sugar after all, but were a type of poison intended for sick animals.

"It was a medicine for animals who get worms in the intestine. It kills the worms. Most of the people who ate these cubes died on the train. They were in terrible pain. Again, luck. Nobody wanted to give me a piece of that."

Why did the prisoners get back on this freight train? Why didn't they use this opportunity the Allied air raid gave them to escape?

Abe responds indignantly: "Escape where? We were in the heart of Germany. I wouldn't take a chance that a German would hide me. I wouldn't trust them. If they were caught the SS men would kill them and me. Also, we'd heard bombs everywhere. Pretty soon we knew there'd be an end to the war. It wasn't going to last years anymore."

Corpses on open rail car of death train

Forced laborers digging storerooms for potatoes

CHAPTER 13

Buchenwald

After withstanding the Allied air attack, Abe's freight train continued on its perilous journey to the Buchenwald concentration camp in east-central Germany. At some point along the way, Abe passed through Gross-Rosen, one of the biggest and most brutal of the Nazi concentration camps. Historical records maintained by the Third Reich reflect that on February 10, 1945, Abe was sent from Gross-Rosen to Buchenwald, where he was assigned prisoner number 129597 (this one was not tattooed on his body).

The route taken by Abe—Auschwitz/Jaworzno to Blechhammer to Gross-Rosen to Buchenwald—was a common one used by the Nazis at the end of the war. As the Nazis became squeezed by the Allied armies in February of 1945, they evacuated prisoners from camps in the vicinity of Allied attacks and the front lines and moved them into central Germany. Consequently, by the time Abe arrived at Buchenwald, the camp was overflowing with prisoners.

"In Buchenwald, there were so many people coming in they couldn't handle it. They came in the thousands because they were shipping in all the prisoners from the East—from Poland, Czechoslovakia—because the Russians were coming."

There was no room in the Buchenwald barracks for Abe and the other passengers who had somehow lived through the Death Marches and the abysmal train rides from Blechhammer and Gross-Rosen.

"It was very crowded so we couldn't get into the camp. So they put up very large tents and we slept in them."

The primitive tents lacked flooring so the prisoners were forced to sleep on the ground in the mud. There were no beds, mattresses or blankets. Even though it was the dead of winter, so many people were packed into the tent that at first the air inside was warm. But during the night, while they slept, it grew bitterly cold. One morning Abe could not get up.

"I was frozen to the ground. A guy next to me took a piece of metal and cut off the back of my clothes so I could get up. From then on, I suffer back pains in my lower spine.

"In Landsberg, Germany [after the war], a doctor said, 'I never saw a man twenty years old with a back like that. You have a back like a seventy-year old. Until today, I have back problems."

Abe describes how the Jewish people slept near each other at night for protection. They knew they could rely on one another so they stayed close while they were sleeping.

"Some of the prisoners would kill you if they thought you had a piece of bread, so the Jews would sleep together as a group in case you needed help."

Did a hungry Jew ever kill another Jew for food?

Abe rubs his chin, dons a rueful smile, then shakes his head. "Bread was life. People were at the point where they'd kill for a piece of bread. You had to get rid of it as soon as possible—not even hold it in your hand. You thought if you eat another piece of bread you live. If you don't eat, you lose weight, you don't have strength. People were dying from hunger. When I got up in the morning we had to be counted. SS men came and counted us. There'd be four or five missing so a prisoner was called to check on the dead people and bring out the bodies. When I was standing in line, plenty of times, I saw people point to a body and heard them say, 'See that guy, he had a piece of bread and during the night someone must have killed him.' I saw fights over soup and bread but I never saw someone being killed for bread."

At the Buchenwald concentration camp, the Nazis did not have any productive work for the prisoners. To keep busy, they were ordered to move things from one spot to another, and then back again.

How did Abe handle the tedium of being forced to perform inane, meaningless work?

"We didn't have any feelings about it. We were ordered to go and we had to do it. No questions."

It wasn't too long before Abe had another near-death encounter at this camp. He tells the story of how one day at Buchenwald a Jewish prisoner "went crazy" and killed a German guard with his shovel, almost decapitating him.

"They started to shoot at the guy who ran behind a pile of wood and was killed immediately. Then they called headquarters and Jeeps came with machine guns and high-ranking officers."

The Nazis customarily used mass reprisals to maintain control over their inmates. In retaliation for the shovel incident, the SS men surrounded hundreds of prisoners with machine guns and forced all of them to stand in a long line, four people deep.

"Within a few minutes, every tenth prisoner had to leave the line, stand against a wall and turn around. Then they were shot in the back."

Abe was number eight.

This is where luck intervened, yet again. But hundreds of others were not so lucky that day.

"If a prisoner killed an SS man, maybe five-hundred Jews got killed for one. They showed us what would happen if we revolted."

———————————————

One evening at Buchenwald, in the middle of the night, SS men pushed inside Abe's tent and aimed flashlights and machine guns at five men. Abe, one of the five, was ordered to rise and follow the menacing guards.

Terrified, Abe thought this was the end of the line for him—surely he had been selected for death. But with armed guards looming over him, he had no choice but to get up and go where he was ordered. He and the four other prisoners were removed from the tent and marched across the icy camp to a barrack surrounded by barbed wire.

Thankfully, Abe quickly learned that this relocation was actually an auspicious move. Instead of being sentenced to death as he'd initially thought, it turned out that he was immensely fortunate to have been one of the select few chosen for this new barrack, known as the Zellenbau. He was now housed with a different caliber of inmates: European political prisoners. He was to share his new quarters with high-ranking officials from France, Russia, Czechoslovakia, and Poland. Leon Blum, the first Jew to serve as Prime Minister of France, Jan Masaryk, the Foreign Minister of Czechoslovakia, and other notable and prominent politicians were among the elite prisoners.

Abe reports that the esteemed residents of this barrack were treated much differently from the other inmates at the camp. They did not go to work and were not asked to perform any type of labor. In fact, they did nothing but sit and eat at a long narrow table and get counted daily by the SS men.

Abe does not know why he was selected to live in this special section, but the time he spent there gave him the opportunity to rest and recuperate. He needed to regain his strength after the Death March and the bullet strike he'd sustained during the train ride from Blechhammer. If not for this recovery period when he was treated like a special prisoner, he may not have made it through the war.

"We didn't do any manual labor. We were a privileged block. We didn't even go every morning for a counting. They chose us because people from that block got killed or died. There was an opening—five beds for five people. Why me? Because an SS man didn't ask. He just said 'You're coming with me!' It was pure, pure luck."

Even in this privileged section, the Jews were discriminated against by their fellow prisoners. Abe recounts the fighting amongst the inmates over care packages.

"I was only there a month or so. When we came in there were very few Jews, mostly Polish men, politicians. They got packages from the Red Cross, but antisemitism was so strong that the *Polaks* and Russians said Jews shouldn't get any of these packages. They said Jews shouldn't get food from the Red Cross because they don't believe in the cross and who would send food for the Jews? The leader in charge of the block, who was a German prisoner, was a very liberal guy and said 'We'll all get them, we're all prisoners.' For non-Jews, it was four guys to a package. For Jews, it was eight guys to a package."

These packages contained sardines, crackers, cheese, and dry bread. Abe cannot help to point out the irony of who packaged the sardines that the antisemitic prisoners tried to keep away from the Jews.

"The funny thing, on the sardine pack, the writing was in Hebrew. It came from Palestine." Palestine was the name of the region in which Israel was founded in 1948.

Interestingly, Abe says some of his fellow prisoners were more generous than others. For instance, the Frenchmen gave more to the Jews, and a few of the Polish prisoners who could communicate with Abe in his own language also gave him more.

"The packages weren't that big so we didn't get very much. We swallowed it so fast we didn't even taste it."

It was only a matter of weeks before Abe and these other prisoners from Buchenwald were transferred to another concentration camp in Germany, near Munich.

"We got Red Cross packages two or three times before we were shipped out to Dachau."

Buchenwald: Exterior view

Crematorium

Row of watch towers surrounding the camp

Barracks (Interior view)

Barracks (Exterior view)

Main gate of the Buchenwald concentration camp.
The sign reads: "To Each What Is His"

Emaciated Prisoners

Original Nazi records

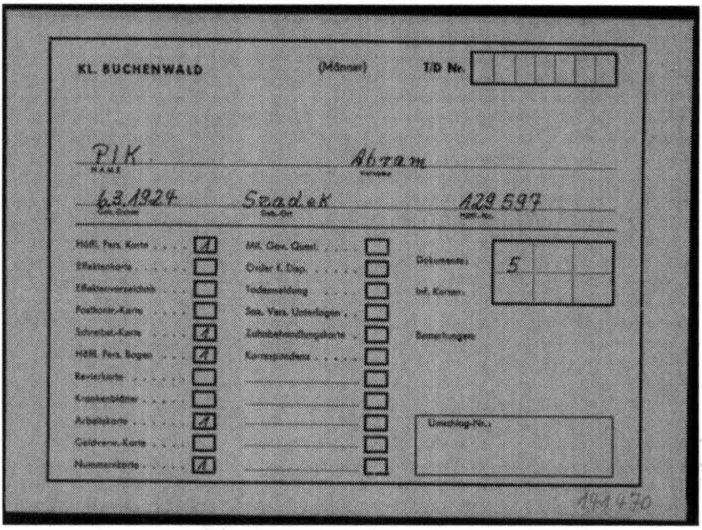

KL. BUCHENWALD (Männer) T/D Nr.

PIK Abram

NAME Vorname

6.3.1924 Szadek 129 597

Geb.-Datum Geb.-Ort Häftl.-Nr.

Häftl. Pers. Karte 1

Effektenkarte

Effektenverzeichnis

Postkontr.-Karte

Schreibst.-Karte 1

Häftl. Pers. Bogen 1

Revierkarte

Krankenblätter

Arbeitskarte 1

Geldverw.-Karte

Nummernkarte 1

Mil. Gov. Quest.

Order f. Dep.

Todesmeldung

Soz. Vers. Unterlagen

Zahnbehandlungskarte

Korrespondenz

Dokumente: 5

Inf. Karten:

Bemerkungen:

Umschlag-Nr.:

141 470

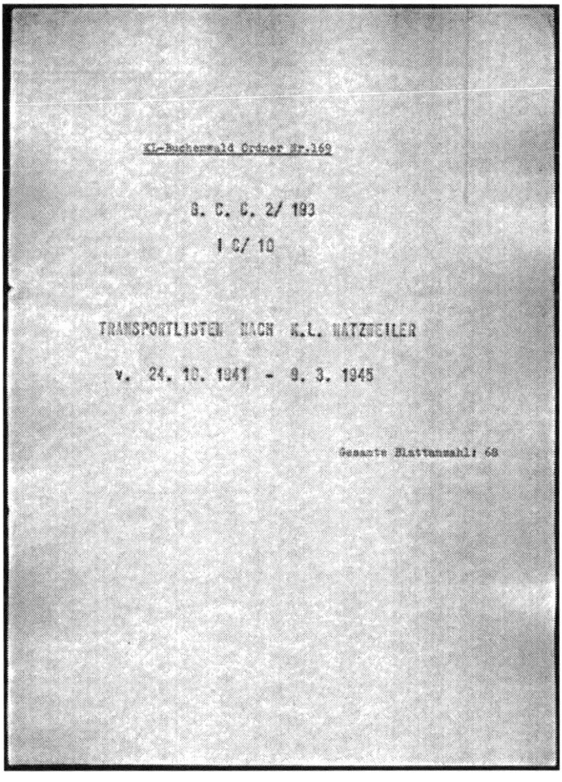

KL-Buchenwald Ordner Nr.169

S. C. C. 2/ 193

I C/ 10

TRANSPORTLISTEN NACH K.L. NATZWEILER

v. 24. 10. 1941 - 9. 3. 1945

Gesamte Blattanzahl: 68

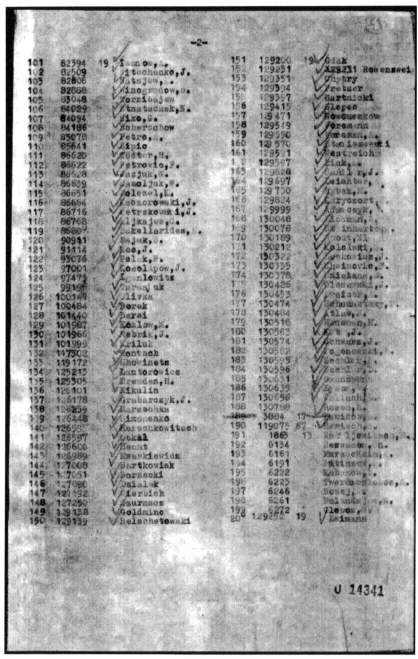

101	82394	19	Iwanow,...	151	129200	19 Ciak
102	82509		Ditschenko,J.	152	129231	X29231 Rosenswei
103	82806		Watajew,..	153	129351	Onytry
104	82888		Winogradow,..	154	129304	Fretzer
105	83048		Korzibajew	155	129397	Bartnicki
106	84029		Ztnatschek,N.	156	129415	Slepec
107	84094		Niko,G.	157	129471	Nowowenkow
108	84186		Koherschow	158	129549	Joromann
109	85078		Petro,..	159	129550	Wroman,..
110	85641		Lipic	160	129570	Boniasewaki
111	86620		Kodter,N.	161	129571	Westreich..
112	86622		Petrovic,P.	163	129597	Fick,...
113	86628		Wasjuk,N.	163	129628	Guhli x,J.
114	86839		Samoljuk,W.	164	129697	Weichter,..
115	86651		Wolexel,h.	165	129700	Rybak,N.
116	86664		Saborowski,J.	168	129824	Kryssort..
117	86716		Petrskowski,J.	167	129999	Simonyk,..
118	86768		Miljkajew,G.	168	130048	Lehmann,..
119	86880		Sakellarides,..	169	130078	Winhart..
120	90941		Bajuk,J.	170	130189	Pout,Wl
121	91114		Loo,J.	171	130212	Koloinki,..
122	95076		Folok,F.	172	130322	Markorius,J.
123	97001		Koselapow,J.	173	130335	Weinovic,..
124	97473		Ignulowitz	174	130378	Wiekamz,..
125	99158		Caruajuk	175	130426	Blamenski,J.
126	100148		Slivka	176	130453	Snaisev,..
127	100484		Borek	177	130474	Schomanney,..
128	101440		Barai	178	130484	Slak,J.
129	101987		Koslow,M.	179	130518	Siemonny,H.
130	101966		Rabnik,J.	180	130563	Ket,J.
131	101999		Criluk	181	130574	Schname,J.
132	117502		Fontaoh	182	130582	Oszonewski,..
133	119172		Khominets	183	130595	Zechlak,J.
134	125213		Lantorowicz	184	130596	Zockl,F..
135	125305		Dresden,H.	185	130631	Ozingdai
136	126101		Mikulin	186	130635	Spaar,..
137	126178		Grabarczyk,J.	187	130656	Gilluch,..
138	126259		Baraschka	188	130708	Rosen,N.
139	126448		Simonenko	189	5884	17 Guminay,..
140	126559		Beraschkowitsch	190	119075	87 Wleniech,..
141	126697		Sokal	191	1869	13 Saf ljewiozo,..
142	126600		Hecht	192	6134	Rewuson,.. G.
143	126989		Kwaskiewicz	193	6161	Murachkin,..
144	127008		Bartkowiak	194	6191	Lttinson,..
145	127051		Borsecki	195	6222	Kabanow,..
146	127090		Bzialek	196	6225	Twerducuhause,..
147	127192		Lierbich	197	6246	Bosaj,..
148	127259		Baurmacn	198	6261	Balandar..
149	127138		Goldmine	199	6272	Slebow,..
150	127139		Belschetowski	200	129252	19 Leimann

U 14341

Abe's name is listed in the second column, twelfth down.
The Nazis inserted a "c" into his surname Pik

CHAPTER 14

Dachau

When the Allied Forces advanced farther into Germany, the Nazis emptied out the barracks and tents of Buchenwald and sent many of their prisoners farther south to the town of Dachau, in the state of Bavaria. Once again, Abe and other malnourished, maltreated prisoners were stuffed into airless cattle cars and deprived of food and water for the entire trip.

Records kept by the Third Reich reflect that Abe did not go straight to Dachau. According to German transport lists, on March 9, 1945, Abe was transferred from Buchenwald to the Natzweiler concentration camp where he remained until April 7, 1945, when he was moved to Dachau.

Dachau was the first regular concentration camp established in Germany by the Nazi regime. It opened in March 1933, only fifty-one days after Hitler came to power as Chancellor. Dachau was a training center for SS guards, and served as the model for the Nazi concentration camp system.

In the beginning of Hitler's reign as Chancellor, only political opponents of the Third Reich were sent to Dachau, but it wasn't too long before many of those whom were considered undesirable, especially Jews, were rounded up and shipped off to this camp.

By the time Abe's transport arrived in Dachau on April 7, 1945, the camp had exceeded its capacity and could not accommodate any more people. There was no housing, no food, and no supplies.

"We were sent by freight cars to Dachau. We couldn't get in. There was no room for us, no food, no nothing. We were in terrible condition. We slept outside the barracks in tents. When I regained my strength in

Buchenwald, I lost it right away. I became a *Muselmann* ... a man very thin, all bones. I couldn't sit."

The first thing Abe did when he arrived at Dachau was to pay a visit to the camp hospital called the *Krankenbau*. In reality, this so-called medical facility was not actually a care center, but was instead a feared place from which visitors did not return.

"If you walked in there ninety percent didn't walk out because they didn't want sick men. They would kill you—you wouldn't go out the back door alive. But my foot was swollen and I could hardly walk."

At the *Krankenbau*, Abe was fortunate in that he was treated by a Jewish prisoner named Dr. Le Vine (a Frenchman), who he recognized from Auschwitz. Dr. Le Vine told him that it was smart to have peed on the wound. Abe also learned from Dr. Le Vine that a piece of his toe had been shot off.

"He took me to a special room and took care of me. He quickly bandaged me, gave me a salve, some pieces of gauze and said, 'Get out of here right now. No one comes in that door and leaves alive. If anyone asks don't tell them you're sick. Tell them you had a message for me.'" Abe ran out of there as fast as he could, evading death once again.

He was only in Dachau a couple of nights before the SS men took the prisoners on yet another Death March to another concentration camp.

"They sent us a few miles away to Allach, a camp near München [Munich]."

Exterior camp view

Camp barracks and watch tower

Inmates standing at roll call

Mass hanging outside Dachau

Door leading to gas chamber entrance

Interior view of gas chamber

Crematorium

Survivors demonstrating operation of crematoria

Human remains in crematoria oven

Pile of prisoners' clothing near crematorium

Piles of deceased prisoners outside of crematorium

Corpses found at liberation-1945

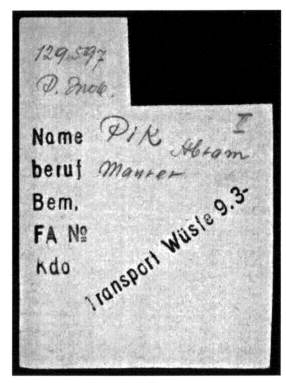

Transport document

CHAPTER 15

Allach

Abe estimates that it took two full days to march the ten miles from Dachau to its largest subcamp, Allach. Even though his toe wound was still healing, he had no choice but to follow the SS men's orders and proceed on the march.

He arrived at Allach on April 12, 1945, where Nazi records show he was given a third prisoner number, 155402. Although this trek from Dachau to Allach was not nearly as high in fatalities as the Death March out of Auschwitz-Birkenau, hundreds of prisoners were shot. And those who survived the march were severely debilitated from extreme hunger and exhaustion.

"People couldn't walk anymore. They were shooting them. More people died than survived the marches. Just to go on living meant that I achieved something. Another day ... another week. You see everyone around you is dying.

"We finally got to Allach in the middle of April [1945]. In Allach, we had plenty of room. The barracks were half empty. People were dying from hunger and disease. Hundreds of bodies were piled up outside against the barracks. The people who were alive were half dead. They fed us once a day. We were worried and angry about not having enough food.

"People weren't buried anymore because there were no people strong enough to do the work. We came and pulled out the bodies. Our job was, whoever died, to *schlep* [drag] them out of the barracks and throw them on the pile. This went on until April 30th [1945]."

On Abe's second or third day at Allach, he saw the SS men packing their things. Most of them ran away as the Allies drew closer.

"We started to feel good when we heard artillery. The main thing was when? How fast? I was hoping the Germans would stop killing us.

"A few days before liberation, SS men were still killing and shooting prisoners, but they were 'less cruel' to prisoners. Normally, when SS men talked we shivered from their iron voices. They didn't holler or hit as much for the few days before liberation. After the war they were wonderful to us."

Abe had heard that the Germans had received orders from Berlin to kill all the Jews as the Allied troops closed in at the war's end.

"But the Germans didn't know how to do it because they were afraid they wouldn't have enough time to bury the dead before America, France, Britain and Russia came and saw what they'd done.

"When they [the Allies] were coming closer, they [the Germans] were trying to cover up the killings. They blew up a couple of crematoria. You could feel it was a few days or weeks before we'd be free. Then a lot of people died, my goodness, because they wouldn't give us any food."

Abe tried to hold on, but without food he knew he was starving to death too. He was so hungry and weak that the short amount of time he spent in Allach—a little over two weeks—felt like an eternity to him. Each day became a race between liberation and death.

He says, "If I was there any longer, I would not have survived. I was so weak … in such bad condition."

Keeping in mind that Abe was one of the first victims of Hitler's reign of terror on Europe in WWII, starting with the Nazis' lightning quick occupation of his hometown of Szadek in September, 1939, it is truly amazing that he made it through the ghetto and then five more years of captivity. By the time Abe ended up in Allach on April 12, 1945, he had survived forced labor and extended imprisonment in a total of nine different concentration and working camps.

But Abe never gave up.

"In the ghetto I wasn't thinking about dying, but in the camps, after a few years, I was thinking if this doesn't end soon we're all going to go. It's just a matter of time. All those years I was losing strength and going down, down. I saw if this goes on long enough, I will not make it. If I wasn't liberated when I was, one week later I wouldn't be here. I felt very bad. I couldn't walk on one leg [because of the gunshot to the toe, which was now severely infected and swollen] and I was very weak. I was skin and bones. All bones."

When Abe peruses photos of grotesquely emaciated Holocaust survivors taken by their liberators, he scowls and grimly declares, "I looked worse than that. I couldn't even stand."

U.S. Army tankmen firing at fleeing Nazi guards

CHAPTER 16

Liberation

In the early morning of April 30, 1945, an American Army tank plowed straight through the front entrance of the Allach concentration camp, mowing down the heavy metal gates and continuing across the camp and out the other side, tearing right through the barbed wire fence.

A wide, heartwarming smile spreads across Abe's face as he remembers this momentous occasion. "I will never forget the American soldiers— our liberators. The Americans were wonderful in all respects."

The Nazi guards and SS men who had remained at the camp immediately retreated. Abe believes it is significant to note that when the Germans fled, he was not aware of any Jews who chased after them to retaliate.

"Jews did not kill the Germans [after they were freed]. I know of no such instances. After the war we could go out and kill Germans—the Americans wouldn't bother us. But two wrongs don't make it right ... I don't want to be a murderer too. I don't know of anybody of the thousands of Jewish survivors who took revenge on the Germans."

Rather than chase the Germans, Abe and some of the other survivors ran out of the camp through the giant tank-sized hole in the back fence to get potatoes which they knew had been buried in the field. The Germans had used the outlying field to store potatoes underground in long furrows during the winter months.

Although Abe was exceedingly weak and had great difficulty walking, he was starving and desperately wanted those potatoes. With bullets flying and American soldiers racing toward him from the woods, Abe limped out onto the field. His mind was set on those potatoes, even if he had to walk through a gun battle to get them.

"The Germans were in the woods shooting and on the other side were the Americans. There were machine guns. You could see bullets popping off left and right at you."

One soldier wearing a uniform that Abe did not recognize—but knew was not German—motioned for Abe to get down. Starving to death, Abe kept going for the potatoes, trying to dig a few out. The soldier in the strange uniform charged at him, yelling in a language he did not understand. Abe had no idea what the soldier was hollering, but the soldier reached him and threw his skeletal frame unto the ground to keep him out of the crossfire.

"When he got me he grabbed me and pushed my head down. He dug a little fox hole with a shovel. He was holding my head because I was lifting my head. And he talks in English and I don't understand a word. He looks at me and says, 'Do you know Yiddish?' He was a Jewish boy—man—eighteen to twenty years old."

It turns out he was an American soldier from Brooklyn. He asked if Abe knew people from his father's town in Poland, but Abe did not.

"That was the first guy I met when America liberated [us]. He was so gracious to me. He didn't know what to do. He gave me all that he had … all the food in his backpack— chocolate, bread—and he said, 'Go back. You're going to get killed. There's still shooting going on.' I remember he pulled out a bottle of wine and pulled out the cork with his teeth and he drank about half of it and gave me the other half."

Abe hobbled back to the camp and devoured all of the food the kind American soldier had handed him, plus some of the raw potatoes he'd managed to dig up. He saved one slice of bread, which he took back to the barracks for a new friend who was too sick to walk. This friend, who lay on the ground because he could not get up, was a man Abe had met during his short stay in Allach. They had instantly connected because the man was from Lask and had known Abe's parents.

"I said to him, 'David', and I gave him the bread in his hand. His eyes opened."

Then Abe left to go to the bathroom because his stomach hurt from all the food he had ingested too rapidly. When he came back he saw that the bread was still in David's hand. Surprised that David had not gobbled up this precious gift, Abe took a closer look at his new friend. He was dead. Heartbreakingly, even though the man had finally been set free, he never got to experience life again outside the hell of the Nazi camp.

Although Abe's first and only thought had been getting to the buried potatoes at the time the American troops tore through Allach, not all of the newly liberated prisoners were thinking about food. Abe chuckles at what was on one fellow survivor's mind.

"On the same day we were liberated, a Jew comes into the barracks and hollers, 'I need ten Jews for a *minyan* [Hebrew for the minimum number (10) of Jewish adults needed for prayer].' A religious Jew was looking for a quorum to *daven* [Yiddish for reciting Jewish prayers]."

Abe clearly recalls that a few hours after the first American tank plowed through the gates of Allach, a second American Army brigade arrived. This brigade was composed of black soldiers whose duties were to care for the survivors. They assessed the condition of the survivors and sent the sick and disabled to an Army field hospital.

"This second brigade of colored troops came in after the first white troops, tanks and army. In World War II, blacks and whites didn't serve together. I had never seen people of color before."

These black American soldiers built showers outside of the prisoners' barracks to bathe the survivors. Abe says he does not know how they did it, but they piped in warm water.

"You have no idea the way we lived—how dirty we were. They put white powder on us—I think it was for killing lice. We were full of lice. They gave us new clothes."

By this point, Abe was in extraordinarily grave condition. Extreme starvation and disease had left him and his fellow inmates in a state of living death. He was so enfeebled and grossly malnourished that he could barely stand. His right toe was also severely infected.

"When we were liberated, the bodies were as high as the barracks. There were more dead than living. I was too weak and drained to rejoice. I could hardly walk. I broke off a piece of the wood from the beds in the barracks to make a cane to hold onto."

Abe had also become very sick from scarfing down the provisions the kind American soldier from Brooklyn had given him, as well as the raw potatoes. His shriveled stomach could not handle the richness and volume of all that food. Another American soldier—a black man—carried him out of the barracks, placed him in a Jeep and drove him from Allach directly to a U.S. Army field hospital in the nearby city of Munich.

"It was a German hospital but the military took it over."

He had terrible diarrhea that was cured over the next seven to ten days in this hospital. In addition, he was completely cleaned up and nursed back to health.

"They shaved me, they cut my hair."

Although Abe did not know English, he knew he was in trouble when a German nun shaved his neck, upper chest and throat one night. He could not understand what she was saying about "tonsils," but he grasped enough to realize he was slated for surgery in the morning.

"She told me in German, 'It's okay, don't worry about it. You're going to get ice cream.'"

Abe was terrified. He thought, "I survived Hitler and now they're going to cut me up? No way!"[5]

He ran from the army hospital in the middle of the night to the neighboring city of Munich. A Jeep with American soldiers drove by and spotted him. Even though he was violating the curfew the military had imposed on Germany, they did not detain him because he was clearly a survivor, still in his *pasiak* (pronounced *pash-ock*, this is the Polish name for the gray and

---

5 Abe still has his tonsils to this day.

black striped prisoner uniform of pants, jacket and hat that Abe was forced to wear in the camps.)

Abe told the soldiers he was looking for other survivors and they dropped him off by a train station in Pasing, a town on the outer edge of Munich. They informed him, "In the morning, a lot of Jewish guys come here."

He waited by himself until morning, when people arrived whom he could communicate with in Yiddish.

"These people saw me in my condition and they said, 'Let me give you a pair of pants, a pair of shoes.'"

One gentleman asked Abe where he was from and when he responded "Szadek," this man informed him that he was from a neighboring town and knew Abe's father and had eaten in his restaurant. This man, also a survivor, had been imprisoned in a K Camp—one of the eleven concentration camps in Kaufering, Germany—and knew people from Szadek who had been liberated and were now living in Kaufering, a small farm village ten to fifteen miles from Munich. Anxious to see other people from his home town, Abe immediately headed to Kaufering.

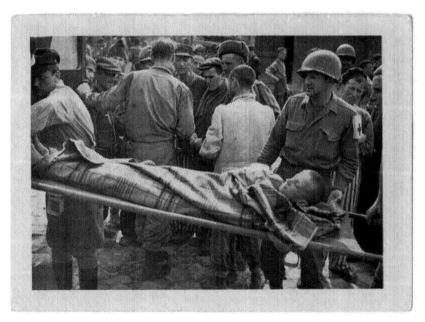

U.S. Army medics help evacuate ill and starving survivors

Liberated prisoners waving American flag

Liberated prisoners greet American soldiers

Liberated prisoner being disinfected

American soldiers view emaciated corpses

CHAPTER 17

Kaufering

As soon as Abe learned that other Holocaust survivors from his hometown of Szadek had taken refuge in the village of Kaufering, Germany, he set out to locate them. The only problem was finding a way to get there.

Fresh out of the American military hospital with no money and no access to any other kind of transportation, Abe boarded a train. When the conductor came through the car to collect the train fare, Abe promptly rolled up his sleeve and showed the conductor the tattooed numbers on his left arm. The conductor did not care—Abe still needed a ticket. Then, to Abe's great surprise, a German citizen stepped forward and paid his fare, something which would never have happened prior to the war's end.

Once on the train, what should have been a short trip turned out to be exceedingly long due to the extensive damage to the region caused by the war. There was no longer a direct train line to Kaufering.

"Getting to Kaufering was a hard journey. Two or three bridges were bombed so the train stopped, we got on buses which went around to another bridge, then back on the train. It took a whole day to go on what was normally a one hour trip."

When Abe finally got off the train, he discovered that the wooden bridge leading to the village of Kaufering had been bombed. He had to cross over a river by carefully traversing a few sparse planks. And since the railroad station was about a mile away from the village, he needed to navigate a narrow footpath through acres of corn and wheat fields to get to the village.

Upon Abe's arrival in Kaufering, he was instantly rewarded for his effort. "I felt better. I was a free man. I could walk, talk, eat … everything changed. The war was over. The Americans helped me. I started to feel good. There were people that knew my family. They took me in and helped me." Abe is referring to five or six of his *landsmen*—fellow countrymen from Szadek—who were already in Kaufering.

"They were happy to see me, I was happy to see them. There were four brothers there. I went to school with one of them, Joe Opetut, who became a big philanthropist after he moved to New Jersey.

"All four [Opetut] brothers were in Auschwitz. Two of the brothers went to Jaworzno, but worked in a different mine than me. The other two brothers went to the Buna Concentration Camp, about fifty miles away. When the Russians came closer, the four brothers were moved to K Camps.

Soon after the war ended, Kaufering became home to mostly male survivors. "Before you knew it, there was a group of fifteen to twenty men living there, not just from my town."

Female companions joined them a short time later as relationships formed. Abe ended up meeting his future wife, Helen, while he lived in Kaufering and they remained there over the next four years.

Right after liberation, most women survivors took shelter in Displaced Persons (DP) Camps established by the Americans. DP Camps were located in nearby Landsberg, less than two miles from Kaufering, and in Turkheim, approximately twelve miles away.

People were considered to be Displaced Persons (DPs) if they had been deported from their native countries. Jewish concentration camp prisoners who had survived the Holocaust were designated as DPs because they were unable or unwilling to return to their homelands. After the war, most survivors learned that their entire families had been murdered, and they, themselves, were in poor physical and psychological condition.

Once liberated, Abe chose not to stay in a DP Camp. He had already experienced more than enough camps in his young lifetime and had no interest in going to another one. He concedes that it would have been advantageous to live in the DP Camps because they provided help to the survivors and met all of their needs, but he was against anything that had the name "camp" in it or even resembled the Nazi-style camps. He and his landsmen decided to reside with private German citizens in Kaufering.

"In Kaufering you were freer. They had farmers, a dairy man. We had almost everything. I used to bring a pound of butter, coffee, and cigarettes to Landsberg and get a pair of shoes. I got a haircut for a few eggs. We got these from the Americans. For coffee and cigarettes, I got a motorcycle from the Germans. I would drive it three quarters of a mile from Kaufering to Landsberg."

Landsberg is the famous city near Munich where Hitler had been imprisoned for treason before his rise to power. In 1923, he led an attempted revolt to overthrow the government in Munich called the "Beer Hall Putsch" which failed, and was sentenced to five years in prison. From his jail cell in Landsberg Castle, he wrote his now famous autobiography *Mein Kampf* (My Struggle).

During the war, Landsberg housed a German military compound. After the war, Landsberg became part of the American occupied zone of Germany. According to Abe, the DP Camp in Landsberg housed about 7,000 DPs and the DP Camp in the neighboring city of Turkheim—which accommodated a sizeable women's concentration camp during the war— had a very large all-women's DP Camp after the war.

Once the war ended, survivors who had lost their entire families found themselves completely alone. Craving human closeness and companionship, many formed relationships very quickly and got married in a short period of time.

"At first, I could not and would not make any plans for my future because I did not know what the future would bring for me. If I found my sister I would've gone where she was. In Kaufering, I became normal again. I was looking for a girl.

"A lot of the men from Kaufering and Landsberg would go to the DP Camp in Turkheim to meet girls. Within six months, sixty to seventy percent of male survivors found female companions. Two of the Oputet brothers went to Turkheim and met two cousins who they married."

Once the Holocaust survivors immigrated to other countries, there was no further need for the DP Camps, so the Landsberg DP Camp closed in 1950.

After World War II, many German residents took Jewish survivors into their homes. The same German people who'd either stood idly by while innocent human beings were slaughtered or who'd enthusiastically supported the Nazis, suddenly wanted to house Jews. Why?

Here is Abe's theory:

"After the war, private German citizens who lived near the camps wanted to show they were not bad people. They wanted to protect themselves by showing the world that they didn't do anything wrong. They would be able to say, 'I have a survivor living with me.'"

He further explains: "After the war, they did it for protection, I call it. They took in a Jew, gave him a room, they helped with food. We got plenty of food, we had rations, food from the DP camps. They liked us, the Germans, because they knew when it came time to look for Nazis, they were Jew lovers. They didn't want to be seen as Nazi helpers … they treated us very well."

Abe believes that German civilians who claimed ignorance about what the Nazis were doing to the Jews during the war were lying. The open brutality and ongoing oppression of the Jews, the discriminatory antisemitic laws, the public roundups, deportations and numerous—over 1,000—concentration camps were all so prevalent in Germany that it was impossible not to know.

Thus, with all of this evidence, Abe becomes infuriated when he discusses how the German citizens denied knowledge of the Nazis' atrocities once the Allies took over. He grits his teeth and his face flushes with anger at the memory of the German people pleading ignorance.

"The minute the war was over, all the Germans knew nothing. The Russians, Americans, British, all blamed the Germans for killing Jews but the Germans were saying: 'We didn't know about it. The government did it. We had Jewish friends.' But they all liked Hitler when he was taking over Poland and France. I blame each and every German … they knew about it. There were very, very few Righteous Gentiles.[6]

"They [German citizens] didn't help [us]. After the war, they couldn't wait for us to leave. They [the Germans] forged records if America wouldn't let you in because you had a criminal record–like being caught in the black market. They [the Germans] would strike it out just to get rid of us."

K Camps

In further support of Abe's contention that German citizens knew full well the Jews were being systematically rounded up, enslaved and slaughtered, he states that the Nazis did not hide what they were doing— they overtly carried out their atrocities for all to see. He cites the tiny farm village of Kaufering as an example of a place where numerous concentration camps were located in plain sight.

In Kaufering—which was so small it had no streets and everyone knew each other's business—Abe maintains that it was impossible not to know what was happening to the Jews. He divulges that within the ten mile radius of Kaufering, there were eleven quite visible, quite prominent concentration camps, all clearly marked. These K Camps were right out in the open. The Nazis, seemingly proud of what they were doing, posted conspicuous signs on the exterior of each K Camp, starting with "Kaufering Concentration Camp I" all the way through "Kaufering Concentration Camp XI."

After the war, while Abe lived in Kaufering, he saw all of the K Camp locations—the Kaufering Concentration Camp signs and fenced-in prisons—for himself. "Some of the K Camps were not far from the train

---

6 *Righteous Gentiles are non-Jews who risked their lives during the Holocaust to save Jews. They are recognized at Yad Vashem, the Holocaust Memorial in Israel, which contains the world's largest repository of information on the Holocaust.

station. I passed them by on a bicycle I got, then a motorcycle. When I was with other survivors, they would say, 'This was my camp.'"

Every few miles there was another K Camp, each of which housed hundreds or thousands of prisoners during the war, depending upon its size. Even with a large number of conspicuous camps in such close proximity, Abe still heard citizens of Kaufering claim they had no knowledge of the K Camps or of the maltreatment of the Jewish people.

Abe maintains that there were big German factories located in Kaufering which required laborers, so the Nazis set up rural concentration camps nearby. The K Camp prisoners were required to work in these factories. When Abe connected with his landsmen after liberation, they told him that they were forced to make airplane parts. Research reveals that these K Camps were specifically created for inmates to build fighter aircraft in reinforced underground factories, out of sight of the Allied bombers.

When Abe's landsmen recounted their horrific tales of captivity in the K Camps, Abe learned that their experiences were quite similar to his. They lived in wretched conditions, were brutally mistreated and subsisted on watery soup. If someone got sick in a K Camp or refused to work, they were immediately shipped off to the nearest concentration camp, Dachau, for execution.

Abe relates that a memorial was erected in Kaufering in 1946 by the Americans to commemorate all those who did not make it through the Holocaust alive.

"We pushed for the memorial. It was a big tombstone constructed by the railroad where Germans would throw bodies off the trains. Most of the people were from K Camps, but there were also bodies collected from the Death Marches and the last days before the war ended. When I first saw it, it was a big grave—the bodies were already buried."

Abe in Kaufering after liberation

Abe & friends. Standing (from left to right): Moshe & Hanka Oputet, David Duwcia & Frank Burakowski. On front of motorcycle, Abe wearing a jacket given by an American soldier, on back, Berack Wishnia

An American soldier walks through the gates of the Kaufering
1 concentration camp on the day of liberation – April 27, 1945

American soldiers view bodies of Kaufering IV prisoners

Abe in Kaufering after liberation

Helen on motorcycle

CHAPTER 18

Survival After The War

After World War II, the Allies provided Holocaust survivors with basic necessities such as food, clothing, and fuel, as well as medical care, counseling, and other vital services. Survivors also received a great deal of support from the United Nations Relief and Rehabilitation Administration (UNRRA).

UNRRA was founded at a forty-four nation conference in 1943 to give aid to liberated countries and World War II survivors throughout Europe. The organization became part of the United Nations in 1945.

As the principal provider of care to survivors, UNRRA supplied emergency aid, distributed food and medicine, restored public services, repatriated displaced persons to their countries of origin, and provided camps for refugees. UNRRA gave Abe and his landsmen ration cards to obtain food, clothes, and other essential items.

"In 1945 and '46, we got ration cards, like a privileged character. We got help from UNRRA. All the four years after the war we were supported by world Jewry—especially the U.S."

Abe explains that in the post-WWII era, ordinary German Mark were practically worthless, so people bartered heavily. They acquired what they needed through a thriving black market. It took until 1948, under Allied occupation, for German currency to be reformed to Deutsche Mark.

"You had to give in all your money [Mark under Hitler] to get Deutsche Mark [also called D-Mark]. Inflation was so high from regular Mark, so to cure it, they [the Allies] deleted Mark and gave out D-Mark.

Every person got a certain amount of D-Mark from the Americans. Money [in Mark] wasn't good so everything was on the black market. I was supported by rationing. In DP camps we got one carton of cigarettes a week. With that carton, I was a wealthy man—I could buy two cows. I used to get coffee from the DP camps. Germans were going crazy for the coffee. You see the suit I was married in? I bought that for a little coffee. We lived by exchanging things."

Abe and several other survivors made a deal with a local farmer to give them one pound of butter each week, along with other desirable items such as cheese and eggs, in exchange for cigarettes. He then traded these farm products to buy the things he needed, such as the motorcycle he used to travel to Landsberg.

German Compensation

Shortly after the war's end, Abe was offered compensation by the Germans but vehemently turned it down. As a young man who had lost almost everyone close to him in his teenage years, the thought of accepting money for the atrocities inflicted upon him and his family was inconceivable.

"The first secretary of the German Republic after the war was a German Jew–Auerbach. He wanted to give me money because I was a teenager when I was in Germany."

Indeed, from 1946-1951, Dr. Phillip Auerbach served as head of the Bavarian State Restitution Office, which had been set up by the Allies to process restitution and indemnification claims for victims of Nazi racial, religious and political persecution. Leading an office which provided financial compensation to Holocaust survivors was a fitting role for Dr. Auerbach since he, himself, had been a prisoner in the Auschwitz concentration camp.

"He [Auerbach] wanted to give me money for losing my parents. I pushed his desk down and ran out and hollered, 'You can't give me enough money for my parents!'" Abe shakes his head as he reminisces. "I was young and wild."

Understandably, Abe had a hard time coping with the heartbreaking realization that his large loving family had been senselessly murdered and he was left all alone in the world. He had spent so many years just trying to survive that he had been unable to grieve the deaths of those whom he loved. Now that he was free, his suffering took on a new form: he had to face a future without his immediate family and almost everyone he cared about. The full weight of his losses was unbearable.

"When I first came out of the camps I started to think about the whole thing. I got mad. I couldn't find none of my family. I had a father, mother, sister, uncles, aunts ... I had fourteen on my father's side, ten on my mother's side, I couldn't find anyone. I was so mad. Look what they did to me! Now I have nobody!

"After the war a lot of people went crazy. When survivors got their strength back they started to realize they were all alone in this world. I have no parents? No family? What does a man do? We were mad, but we didn't hurt nobody."

Witnessing the torture, enslavement and murder of so many of his people made Abe question his faith and the motives of everyone around him. Helplessly trapped in the insidious camps, feeling completely abandoned by humanity, Abe yearned to be saved from the genocidal hands of the Axis powers for five years, but no rescuer materialized.

"In the camps, I thought, where was God? Why did he tell me to pray every day? It's a lie. Where was America? No one came to help us. I had rage about everyone. Germans would say [after the war] they were friendly to everybody, but the whole country [under the Third Reich] said 'Heil Hitler!'"

Abe was not alone in his indignation. He relates that his fellow survivors experienced similar feelings.

"The young people were so mad. Nothing could stop us. We did dangerous things, got a motorcycle. I settled down a lot when I met Helen. You see, if I wanted to live, I couldn't stay the way I was. I had to go on with my life. I love people. I made a success in business because I was nice to people."

Abe and his landsmen ultimately calmed down and banded together so they could receive assistance from the Jewish social service organization *Hajas* (pronounced *hi-us*).

"In order for us to get help from the *Hajas*, we had to form a committee. Before you know it there was a group of fifteen to twenty of us. We got a president—he was the oldest, in his forties—he was from my town. He remembered me, remembered my parents. I was very active in school. I was a good student. They wanted me to be secretary. I'd take minutes ... do all the secretary's work. I was secretary till I came to the U.S. in 1949. By that time each man was married and had children. I put in a lot of time reading, writing, arithmetic. I had all the papers, kept records. We were a group of survivors. At our highest time we were forty to fifty people."

Interestingly, the president of Abe's committee, named Burakowski, had married a non-Jew back in Poland five to six years before the war. Because his marriage to a non-Jew had not been well-received in Szadek, he'd moved to Lodz. His wife was a professional—a pharmacist—and they had no children together. Once the war began, only Burakowski, not his wife, was taken away to a concentration camp—a K Camp in Germany. After the war, the couple moved to Israel where they lived out their lives.

Post-war Housing & Health Issues

In Kaufering, Abe discovered that he had an uncle—his fathers' youngest sister's husband—who had survived. This uncle, Frank Burakowski, took Abe into his house along with another boy, Hamel Burakowski. Hamel, a fellow survivor, had a serious girlfriend, but he died of lung cancer a few months after liberation.

"He was coughing, spitting up blood, from the camps. He didn't smoke. He was younger than me—he was only eighteen. A lot of survivors died after the war because of health problems from the camps. They were so undernourished, ate too much, then got very sick, had lung problems …"

After the war, Abe also lived with two brothers who had been the victims of the Angel of Death—Josef Mengele—during their incarceration in Auschwitz-Birkenau. While Abe was in Auschwitz, he was unaware of the medical experiments which Mengele had been performing on his fellow prisoners. Although Mengele was known for his experiments on twins, these non-twin siblings were two of Mengele's many subjects.

"He took the brothers and sterilized them. They had a special section for experiments. They took children and men and did horrible things to them. We all felt sorry for these brothers. Almost all of the men got a girlfriend, got married, had a baby, and these brothers were single."

Abe kept in touch with the brothers for a short time after they came to America.

"I talked to them on the phone. They moved around a lot. They got married here and moved farther west. They were much older than me—they were in their forties."

Abe, himself, had ongoing medical problems as a direct result of his time in the camps. Some of these ailments have plagued him for his entire life.

"In Munich, there was a secretary [Dr. Auerbach] to make good to the people that suffered. After the war, I was complaining about my back. It was very bad. The Germans sent me to see a German doctor there. Also, part of my big toe was cut out on the right foot. And there's varicose veins on my legs."

Another major problem Abe experienced shortly after his arrival in Kaufering was that his teeth fell out. He relates that a lot of other survivors suffered a similar loss of their teeth due to severe malnourishment and maltreatment as Nazi prisoners.

"My teeth were falling out by themselves. I went to a German dentist in Landsberg. He gave me something to swallow—I think vitamins—and told me what to eat. He said my gums were too weak and didn't have enough nutrients. In America, I got a check from Germany to fix my teeth."

As for Uncle Frank, he met another woman in Kaufering. His first wife—Abe's aunt—had been murdered by the Nazis.

This new woman took an immediate dislike to Abe. He believes it was because he was part of Frank's first wife's family, so after three to four months of living with Uncle Frank, Abe moved out into the home of a ranger.

In the ranger's house he had a beautiful room and was well-fed. However, he lived with the ranger and another survivor for only a short time because this other survivor had a girlfriend who regularly stayed over, but did not want anyone to know of her premarital sexual activity. To escape this awkward living arrangement, Abe left the ranger's home to move in with a farmer.

Abe & Landsmen (Abe on far right, bottom)

Abe (on left) with Hamel Burakowski & friend

Abe in Kaufering

CHAPTER 19

Helen

In the Nazi camps, men and women were imprisoned separately. Teenagers and young adults, like Abe, found themselves unnaturally alienated from members of the opposite sex for many years.

Thus, after liberation, it did not take much time before each of Abe's landsmen found girlfriends. They had been deprived of female companionship for so long that they were each quick to find an available lady.

"In the camps, we never had contact with women. They got off the trains and were taken away. I learned a little after the war. The [normal] way teenagers live today [mixing with other genders], I did not have. I didn't see a girl all those years. You didn't see a woman, talk to her, touch her..."

Abe lived in Kaufering about ten months before he entered into a serious relationship with a woman, Helen, whom he met through another survivor named Harry Goodman. Harry had been liberated from one of the K Camps and was much older than Abe. He'd been married before the war and was a successful businessman, owning a dye factory in Lodz, Poland.

After the war, Harry had returned to Poland but learned very quickly that there was no future for him there. In the early spring of 1946, he came back to Kaufering accompanied by a pregnant wife and her two single sisters. One of these sisters, Helen, became Abe's wife.

Abe's eyes light up and there's an endearing smile in his voice when he talks about the first time he met Helen: "She was very cute. So loveable.

We talked, then we got closer. She had two curls on the sides," he says, pointing near his ears. "I fell in love with her."

When Abe and Helen first met, he was twenty years old and she was nineteen. Like him, she was a Polish survivor who had lost almost everyone in her family. Born in Belchatow on September 10, 1925, she was one of seven children—three girls and four boys—of whom only she and her sisters Regina and Salah survived the Nazi carnage. Her parents, extended family, and all male relatives were killed, including her beloved younger twin brothers.

Pre-war Belchatow had been a prospering city in Poland with over 30,000 Jews. Tragically, only 1% made it through the Holocaust. It is nothing short of a miracle that Helen and both of her sisters survived when 99% of the Jewish citizens of Belchatow were murdered.

Abe says that Helen and her two sisters never wanted to talk about the horrors they had witnessed and the suffering they had endured. Here is what he does know:

During the war, Helen and her family were forced into a ghetto in Belchatow from October 1, 1939 through June, 1942. From there, she, Regina, and Salah were moved to the Lodzer ghetto, where they remained for one year until June, 1943. Then, they were sent to Auschwitz for two months, until August, 1943, when they were relocated to another concentration camp called Marzdorf, in East Germany.

After being held captive for a total of five and a half years, Helen and her two sisters were finally liberated from Marzdorf by the Russians in early 1945. Abe believes Helen's liberation occurred during January of that year.

His recollection is most likely accurate in that the United Nations established International Holocaust Remembrance Day on January 27th to globally commemorate the anniversary of the date Soviet troops liberated Auschwitz-Birkenau in 1945. The remainder of the Nazi camps were liberated over the next several months by the Allied troops.

Abe never learned much about the three sisters' day-to-day experiences in the ghettos and camps other than the fact that they were forced to work in a knitting factory. All Helen ever really told him was that she was up to her knees in water all the time.

He does know that after Helen and her sisters were liberated by the Russians, they returned to Poland. Since they were not welcome back in their homeland, they did not stay very long.

"The Russians did not help them after the war. They just said, 'You're free.' They were liberated a few months before me. They didn't put women in DP camps [at first] so they told them to go home. So they went back to Poland to look for their family. That's where Helen's older sister, Salah, met her husband, Harry Goodman. Then after eight or nine months they went to Kaufering because Poland was so antisemitic. There were pogroms. When Jews came back and wanted their houses and property back the Poles killed them."

Abe had also wanted to return to his homeland to search for family members and remnants of his former life but was advised against it.

"I met a landsman who said to me, 'Don't go there. There's nothing there … nobody. Stay here. They'll kill you if you go there.'"

Engagement

Although Abe initially liked Helen, he did not want to marry her. He thought Helen was far too religious for him, since he was not religious at all.

"We liked each other but she came from a very, very religious family. They wouldn't eat anything before they said a prayer."

He discussed his concerns with Helen and she said they would compromise. But Abe had grown up with some extremely religious relatives of his own, so he anticipated a fair amount of turbulence. He told her: "Even if we have an argument, we'd make up before we went to bed."

Abe related his reservations to his older cousin, Arje (pronounced *Aria*) Najman, a thirty-two year old survivor who lived near him in Kaufering. Arje, the son of Abe's mother's brother Shmuel, had escaped occupied Poland by running away to Ukraine. As difficult as it is to comprehend that he left behind a young wife and two little boys in Poland, Abe explains that "there came a time when either he left or they'd all get killed." And, in fact, Arje's wife and sons were murdered.

Arje, a deeply religious man, feared that Abe would marry a non-Jew. When Abe expressed his doubts about Helen, Arje asked to meet her. When he did he was truly impressed. He told Abe: "When are you going to meet someone like her again? What do you want? You can't get a better girl. You should marry her."

Abe thinks his cousin Arje really liked Helen because she knew how to *daven* (say prayers in Hebrew).

"In those days girls went to public [primary] school but not high school. Helen learned Hebrew prayers at home from her father and four brothers, and she went to *Bet Jacob* [a private orthodox school for girls]. When I met her she was very religious."

One by one, Arje shot down each of Abe's concerns about getting married. When Abe argued that he and Helen could not get married because they had no rabbi, Arje said he would find them one.

When Abe countered that they could not get married because he had no money and they needed a meal, Arje responded, "Don't worry, I'm going to make you a wedding."

As luck would have it, Helen's sister Regina *(Rifka)* also had a serious boyfriend at the time, but did not have money for a wedding either. Arje said he would marry all of them together, so the two couples decided to get married in a double wedding.

Abe relates that getting married jointly was an easy decision for the two sisters. "Helen and Regina were only a year apart. They were very close—like twins. They went to school together."

However, before Abe could plan a wedding he needed to get engaged, which meant he needed to buy a ring. Without money, though, he had to be creative.

"In 1946, in Germany, money was no good. You had to barter. Don't ask me what I traded—a couple of pounds of butter, coffee, cigarettes—the ring was made from some kind of iron or wire."

Inflation was so high in Germany after WWII that even if Abe had any money it would have been impractical to use.

"People carried their money around in bags and briefcases because everything cost so much. A pound of butter was 1,000 Mark. Money wasn't worth anything. We lived by exchanging things. This is before they changed the money—Mark under Hitler—to the Deutsche Mark. When Americans came, all German Mark were worth nothing. Then Deutsche Mark came out."

In order to make the wedding, Abe found a way to overcome all of his major obstacles. First, he needed to serve food but had no money to purchase any. Ever-resourceful, Abe and his future brother-in-law—also named Abe (Burowski)—approached a local farmer and traded him American cigarettes and coffee for a cow. In the village, the butcher agreed to allow them to use his space to kill the cow.

But now they faced their next big problem: They needed a kosher butcher—a *shochet*—to kill the cow in a certain way to make it kosher. Fortunately, Abe's cousin Arje was able to find one.

Another considerable challenge was outfitting the bride and groom. Helen needed a wedding dress, but they had no means to buy one. Where would they get a fancy, expensive dress without any money living in the tiny farm village of Kaufering?

They ultimately borrowed one from a dressmaker in the nearby city of Landsberg. The one condition was that it had to be returned the morning following their wedding.

And what would Abe wear?

He cleverly traded the coffee and cigarettes he was given by an American soldier to buy a navy blue wedding suit for himself.

"It was a used suit from a German which I wore to my wedding and brought with me to the U.S."

Finally, when all the wedding hurdles had been surmounted, Abe found himself in jail.

Jail

Less than a week before the wedding, a friend frantically awoke Abe at two o'clock in the morning yelling, "The MPs [Military Police] are taking the meat away!"

Abe raced over to the butcher shop in the village of Kaufering where his slaughtered cow was being stored and tried to stop the American MPs from confiscating his meat. He shouted at them, "You can't take this meat! This is for my wedding!" The MPs asked, "Is this your meat?" He replied, "Yes," and they said, "So you come with us too."

The MPs took both Abe and the cow meat down to military head-quarters under the presumption that Abe was trying to sell the meat illegally. Because food was limited and rationed after the war, there was a huge black market, and the MPs believed Abe was engaging in criminal activity.

Abe was taken to Landsberg Prison—the same jail where Hitler had written *Mein Kampf*—but states that he did not go quietly. This was the Monday before his wedding and he screamed and yelled, "I'm getting married on Sunday!"

The MPs did not listen to his passionate defense so he spent the night in jail. The following morning, Captain Trot—a short, cigar-smoking American Army officer— came in to speak to him. Apparently, Captain Trot needed to decide what to do with Abe but understood little German. Trot asked Abe if he spoke Yiddish and Abe quickly learned that Trot was a second generation Jew from America.

Trot questioned him, "What's the story? You're in the black market?"

Happy that he could communicate with this man, Abe responded, "What black market? I'm getting married on Sunday and in a wedding you need food. I'm inviting people ... I sent out invitations."

Abe happened to have one of his wedding invitations in his shirt pocket and showed it to Trot as proof that he was not doing anything illicit with the cow. He even invited Trot to the wedding. Thankfully, Trot believed Abe's wedding story and released him, instructing two MPs to drive him back to Kaufering—with the cow meat.

Captain Trot personally made an appearance at the double wedding to confirm the veracity of Abe's story. Abe has always remembered the kindness and understanding of Captain Trot, and instantly recognized his name when he recently read in a local North Jersey newspaper that Trot had died. From Trot's obituary, Abe officially learned that this compassionate man had been in charge of the MPs in Landsberg after the war.

Helen & Abe in Kaufering

Helen after the war

Helen with sisters Regina & Salah

CHAPTER 20

A Wedding & A Baby

The Wedding

Abe and Helen's wedding invitation was printed in Yiddish. "AJNLADUNC" across the top meant "Invitation." The text, translated to English, read:

We have the honor of inviting you to our weddings which will be on Sunday November 3, 1946 at 8:00
Helen Fajwelman   Regina Fajwelman
Abe Pik   Abram Brzegowski

Both couples sent their invitations to the numerous friends they had made in the camps, but there were also many wedding crashers who attended their double celebration.

"Everybody came. The people I didn't invite that knew me—they came anyway. We had a festive wedding."

Abe estimates that they had at least one hundred people in their big hall—called the *Comitate*—in Kaufering, which they obtained through the Jewish Community Council.

"We got a big place over a bar—a *Bierstuberl* [beer hall]. The guy downstairs catered it. We played cards in this room ... came here every day. This is where the bris [for Jack] was. These were our happiest days without money."

Sadly, however, with almost all of Helen and Abe's family members murdered, the wedding ceremony served to underscore just how alone in the world the bride and groom really were. Traditionally, parents, grandparents, siblings, aunts, and uncles participate in a wedding ceremony, but Abe and Helen had to substitute other people. It goes without saying that their guest list was composed almost entirely of friends.

"We didn't have any close relatives at the wedding. Helen's sister Salah couldn't come to the wedding because she was in the hospital having a baby [Berta, born October 31, 1946]. My closest relative was my cousin, Arje. To go under the *chuppah* [the canopy under which a Jewish couple gets married–symbolizing the home they will build together], you need a man and a woman. Arje was very religious and said my other cousin Ruth [who married twelve months earlier] couldn't go under by Jewish law because she was pregnant. Normally, your parents would take you. I got another couple from Szadek to take me—they were husband and wife."

After a joyous evening of delicious food and great music, it was too late for most of Abe and Helen's guests to return to their homes due to the military curfew which had been imposed upon Germany—an interdiction only lifted two years later. Thus, their guests stayed all over their house, including their bedroom, giving them a rather unconventional wedding night.

"After the wedding we didn't have any time together. People were sleeping on the floor. We slept with twenty-five people in my room ... tell that to an American couple!"

Abe proudly holds up his only wedding picture, an eight by ten faded sepia photograph of the bride and groom. Helen is wearing her beautiful borrowed dress, with a raised flower in the center of the chest and a long, lacy veil cascading to the floor. Since the dress had to be returned the Monday morning following the wedding, the happy couple stopped at a professional photographer to have this solitary wedding photo taken on the way to drop off the dress in Landsberg.

Abe's eyes sparkle and his entire face brightens as he talks about the blissfully carefree time he and Helen spent together after their wedding.

"I had a wonderful honeymoon. We went to a town in the Alps called Berchtesgaden [Germany]. Hitler had a castle over there. That's the most gorgeous country that you can see. We went up there with a cable car. There was a hotel on top. Germans weren't allowed to go up there. It was only for the military and people without a country—called *Staatenlose,* in German. I showed them my DP identification ... I had no money. Everything I got for free.

"We went back to Kaufering for a few weeks after the honeymoon and then traveled again for a whole year. We went to all the DP camps in Germany. Helen and I had friends at every camp—we found people we knew or who knew people we knew."

Abe easily recites each of the DP camps he and Helen visited as newlyweds: "Landsberg, Gross-Rosen, Bad Reichenhall, Turckheim, Bergen-Belsen and Feldafing." The last DP camp closed in 1957.

"We had the most wonderful time of our lives because we didn't have to worry about money. It was the best time of my life when I didn't have a penny to my name. We had ration cards. We traveled by train but we didn't pay. When the conductor would come over you would say 'I'm a Jew' and you could ride. If a conductor insisted we pay, a German would pay for us. Before that, if you said you were a Jew, they'd arrest you. We were a bunch of privileged characters."

Baby Jack

Life was simple and untroubled for Abe and Helen in the early years of their marriage. The Americans and UNRRA provided them with sufficient food, clothing, and medical care to meet all of their needs, and they lived for free with a local farmer. Abe remembers their first address: "House #125, Kaufering, Germany." He explains that there was no street name because there were no roads in Kaufering at that time.

The young couple lived together for several years before they had a child. Deeply scarred by the atrocities committed against their people, particularly the Nazi murder campaign against children, they were fearful of bringing a Jewish baby into the world.

"After I got married, I was very hesitant to have a child. I was afraid. I just saw a million and a half children killed. I saw my cousin being taken away because he was young. Finally we saw other people having children. My son was born three years after the wedding."

Abe and Helen's only child, Jacob (Jack) Pik, was born in a hospital in Landsberg, Germany, on March 24, 1949. The new parents honored each other's families in the selection of Jack's name.

"We decided when Jack was born we'd name him after both our fathers: Jacob Eliezer [Leo]." Jacob was the name of Abe's father and Eliezer was Helen's.

Abe greatly enjoys recounting the tale of Jack's birth, brimming with delight when he relates the story of the day Jack was born: "The hospital was walking distance to Kaufering. They wouldn't let me into the hospital when Jack was born. The nuns said, 'You can only come in after she gives birth.'

"I went to see Helen and she says in Yiddish, 'Oh, what an ugly kid we've got.' Jack was born yellow so the doctor said you have to wait one month for a bris."

Abe grins widely, "He was such a beautiful baby!"

The birth of a Holocaust survivor's baby was a special occasion which was recognized by UNRRA, *Hajas,* and the Americans in post-WWII Germany. According to Abe, *Hajas* was the organization which helped him and Helen the most after Jack was born.

"If your wife had a baby, you got something special. They did everything for the survivors. They gave us supplies—diapers, clothing, food—helped wash everything …"

U.S. military headquarters in Landsberg, Germany

Abe & Helen with friends in Kaufering

Abe & Helen's only wedding photo

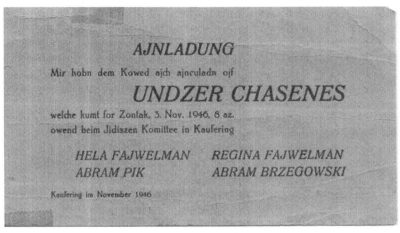

AJNLADUNG

Mir hobn dem Kowed ajch ajnculadn ojf

UNDZER CHASENES

welche kumt for Zontak, 3. Nov. 1946, 8 az.
owend beim Jidiszen Komittee in Kaufering

HELA FAJWELMAN   *REGINA FAJWELMAN*
ABRAM PIK   *ABRAM BRZEGOWSKI*

Kaufering im November 1946

Abe & Helen's wedding invitation

Helen & Abe's first New Year's card

Helen & Abe (far left) at their friends' wedding

CHAPTER 21

Emigrating

Abe, his landsmen and their wives lived with farmers in Kaufering, Germany, until they emigrated to other countries. The majority of couples Abe and Helen knew went to Israel and the United States, some to Australia and Canada, and a few to Belgium and South America. None returned to Poland.

Appallingly, Jewish Holocaust survivors who had been deported from Poland and miraculously escaped Hitler's death sentence were not welcome back in their homeland. If they were fortunate enough to survive years of oppression, torture, and imprisonment at the hands of the Third Reich, they put their lives at risk if they tried to return home.

"Polish Jews came to Germany in 1945 and '46 because there were pogroms back in Poland. After the war, the Polish didn't want the Jews coming back because they had their houses and their possessions so they killed them."

Abe learned about the pogroms from Polish survivors who had gone back to their homes after the war and then returned to Kaufering to report to their fellow countrymen the maltreatment they had experienced.

Without Poland as an option, the most popular destination for Abe's landsmen was Palestine. But prior to 1948, before Israel existed, Palestine was under the control of Great Britain—and the British weren't opening the door for survivors.

"Right after the war, all the survivors wanted to go to Israel, but the British in charge of Palestine wouldn't let the Jews in. The British intercepted the boats carrying the Holocaust survivors from the DP camps in Germany, turned them back, and dropped them on the island of Cyprus in the Mediterranean. The British sent all the Jews to Cyprus until Israel became a state."

It is significant to note that the British did not just drop Holocaust survivors trying to sail to Palestine onto this small island off the southern coast of Turkey; they imprisoned tens of thousands of them in internment camps. In these barbed wire camps on Cyprus—all too reminiscent of Nazi concentration camps—conditions were extremely harsh. The inmates had to endure overcrowding, inadequate food, and a lack of fresh water. They also had to live in cramped tents and barracks.

Britain operated these internment camps from August, 1946 until February, 1949. Pursuant to an overly strict British immigration quota, only a tiny number of these detainees were allowed to enter Palestine each month. Thus, the very same survivors of years of Nazi brutality were re-victimized at the hands of the British while they were held against their will on this Mediterranean island. It took many months after Israel officially became an independent state—on May 14, 1948—for the last group of detainees to leave Cyprus.

Coming To America

Once World War II was over, tens of thousands of displaced Jewish Holocaust survivors with no homes or families were prohibited from entering the United States due to extremely strict immigration restrictions. Aware of the harsh American policies, Abe did not have high hopes for emigrating to the U.S.

"Each country had a quota. I was told that this quota was already taken for years in advance. Only people who had relatives here [in the U.S.] could get here without the quota. The Polish quota was that only 2,000 [people] could come to the U.S. each year."

Fortunately, President Harry Truman was a strong advocate for a liberal immigration policy toward Displaced Persons (DPs) and issued an executive order on December 22, 1945 known as the Truman Directive which established quotas for more DPs to be allowed entry into the U.S.

Immigration quotas were further increased in 1948 when Congress passed legislation allowing 400,000 DPs to enter the U.S. However, this new law was deceiving in that on its face it appeared to be favorable to Holocaust survivors, but the reality was that it heavily favored European agricultural laborers. Consequently, only twenty percent of the 400,000 DPs allowed to come to the U.S. were Jewish immigrants. President Truman called the law "flagrantly discriminatory against Jews." The result was that most of the Jewish DPs went to Israel. It took until 1950 for Congress to amend this law.

Of the handful of Abe's cousins who survived, most went to Israel after the United Nations passed a resolution calling for the establishment of a Jewish state. The Israeli Declaration of Independence was proclaimed on May 14, 1948.

Given the choice of leaving Germany for Israel or America, Abe would have also elected to go to Israel but for unfavorable reports from his cousins who had traveled there first. They wrote him letters while he lived in Germany advising him not to come to Israel because of the terrible conditions there.

"People lived in tents, there was no housing because they came in the thousands … there wasn't enough food. One of my cousins, a female who lived in a tent, had a nervous breakdown there. They wrote that I should go to America so I could help them."

Another factor in Abe's decision-making was that Israeli officials would not let him and Helen emigrate to Israel at that time due to Helen's pregnancy. Abe recalls that in the end of 1948, Israeli Prime Minister Ben Gurion personally visited the DP camps in Landsberg, Germany, to invite the young survivors to Israel, "but the minute they found out Helen was pregnant they wouldn't take me." They told Abe to leave after Helen had the baby "because they needed able bodies to fight."

Without Israel as a viable option, Abe and Helen decided to go to America. Again, they were advised to wait until after their baby was born.

"I was told by the American Consulate that if the baby was born after Helen and I got our visas then the baby couldn't come with us because the baby needed a visa with his name and date of birth. The process would've taken longer, so I waited until Jack was born to register to come to the U.S."

After Helen gave birth to Jack on March 24, 1949, the Piks needed to find a sponsor. At that time, every emigrant needed a sponsor family or organization in order to be allowed entry into the United States. The Jewish Community Council—now called The Jewish Federation—sponsored Abe, Helen, and their six-month-old son, Jack.

The Piks were very fortunate in that they were flown to the U.S. and did not have to endure a long trip at sea like the majority of refugees.

"Most of the people that came to Bremerhaven [a German seaport] went to the U.S. by military boats. Only pregnant ladies and couples with babies under six months were flown. Jack was born March 24, 1949, so he was just six months."

On September 30, 1949, at twenty-four years old, Abe took his first step onto American soil. Having survived the unthinkable and beaten the most improbable of odds, he and his young family were about to begin their lives anew as free people in a free country filled with promise.

———————————

Certain states in the U.S. readily opened their doors to Holocaust survivors. Michigan and New Jersey were two of them.

Originally, Abe, Helen, and Jack were assigned to emigrate to Michigan. However, before they departed for America, Abe informed the German officials that he did not wish to go to Michigan. They instructed him to wait until he reached the United States to change his family's final destination. As soon as he arrived in New York, Abe told the caseworkers from the Jewish Community Council that his wife's sister lived in New

Jersey, her husband worked in textiles, and they wanted to live in New Jersey to be close to them.

Abe is not sure how the Jewish Community Council accomplished it—he thinks they might have switched his family's visa with another family's—but he, Helen and Jack got to remain in New Jersey. Through a recent online search on the National Archives and Records Administration website, Jack was able to find the original Air Passenger Manifest reflecting that he and his parents were initially slated to go to Michigan. Utilizing this website, he was also able to access the records of the Immigration and Naturalization Service—now called U.S. Citizenship and Immigration Services—to obtain his family's 1949 Emigration Cards from Munich.

When Abe first came to America in 1949, he reports that President Truman was allowing 200,000 survivors to enter the U.S. As luck would have it, when he, Helen, and Jack landed, their arrival was a newsworthy event.

"I was told I was the 100,000th immigrant. There was a whole ceremony for us when we got off the plane. They were looking for a young couple with a child. There was a whole write-up in the American paper. There were big shots there. I didn't understand a word of English. I didn't know what was going on. I was supposed to get a present—a watch—which I never got."

After the Piks left the airport, they were sent to a hotel in New York City. Abe remembers the name and location: The Marcel Hotel on 103rd Street and Broadway. They stayed there for one to two weeks until their destination papers were changed.

Once the paperwork was complete, Abe and his small family were sent by bus from the Port Authority Bus Terminal in Manhattan to Paterson, New Jersey, where his case worker, Rose Batavia, picked them up and took them to the Jewish Community Council's office located at 45 Church Street.

"The Paterson Jewish Community Council was a very active organization. There were a couple of hundred DPs here."

At this Paterson office, Ms. Batavia handed Abe $18.75 as spending money and directed him and his family to their new home in America: a furnished room in a woman's house in Paterson.

Abe was overwhelmed by the tremendous amount of kindness bestowed upon him. But as grateful as he was to be given a fresh start in a new land, he was determined to make it on his own. He no longer wished to be the recipient of handouts.

"I was told to come every week to the Paterson Jewish Community Council to get $18.75. I cried that night. I was now in America, but I did not want to receive any more charity. I wanted to support myself and my family, not charity."

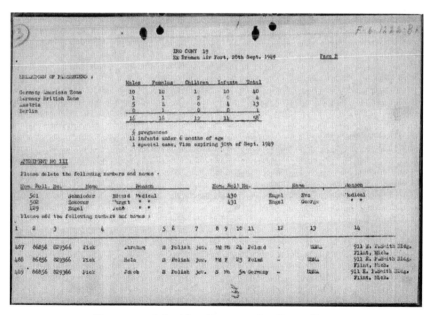

Passenger Manifest Bremen Air Force Base

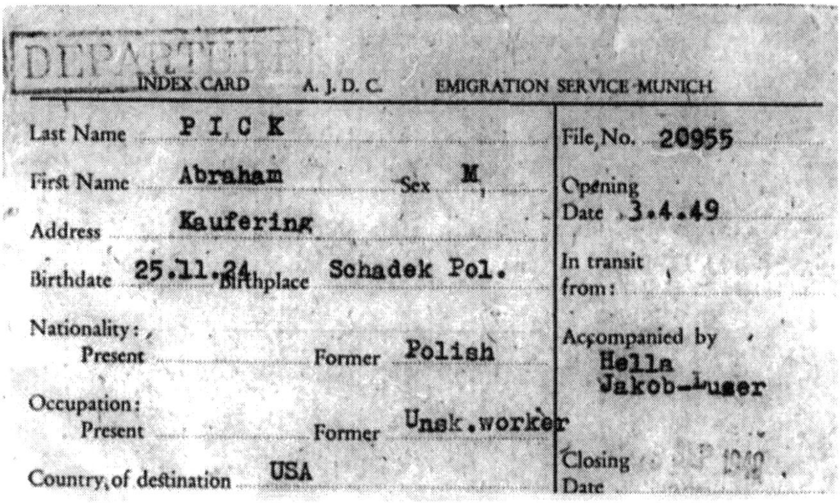

DEPARTURE

INDEX CARD A. J. D. C. EMIGRATION SERVICE MUNICH

Last Name P I C K

First Name Abraham Sex M

Address Kaufering

Birthdate 25.11.24 Birthplace Schadek Pol.

Nationality:
Present Former Polish

Occupation:
Present Former Unsk.worker

Country of destination USA

File No. 20955

Opening Date 3.4.49

In transit from:

Accompanied by
Hella
Jakob-Luser

Closing Date

Emigration Card for Abe

CHAPTER 22

Starting Over in the USA

Abe found work the very next day after he moved to New Jersey. A landsman helped him get a job making kitchen sets called "crumb furniture." His pay was seventy-five cents an hour.

"My first job I did not like. I worked with sulfuric acid, chemicals … I once lost my pants. I had to wear a rubber apron, rubber gloves, and rubber boots and I forgot to wear the apron. I had to clean the chrome so I touched the acid along the belt line of my pants and it cut completely through the material. My pants fell off."

After completing one full week of work, Abe came home to what he believed was bad news. Helen informed him that someone from the Paterson Jewish Community Council (Paterson JCC) had stopped by to see him and left instructions that he needed to report to their office immediately. Abe was terrified to go to the Paterson JCC because he thought the organization wanted him to return the $18.75 he was given his first day in America—which he could not.

"I said to Helen, 'I bet they want the money back.'"

Helen pleaded with him to go, fearful that if he did not they would be arrested or sent back to Germany.

Abe ultimately listened to Helen and went to the Paterson JCC's office the following morning. When he arrived, he found a Yiddish translator and explained to his case worker, Rose Batavia, that it would take him a long time at seventy-five cents an hour, but he would pay them back. Rose laughed when she heard his speech and through the Yiddish interpreter informed him that she did not want the money back. But she did tell him, "When he makes it here he can pay it back then." Abe jokes, "I'm still paying it back."

From his discussion with Rose, Abe learned that he could return to the Paterson JCC's office each week to receive $18.75. This was the amount of weekly support money the agency provided to every survivor.

But Abe was too proud to accept any more of the JCC's money.

"I never went back. I got a job."

Rose also advised Abe that the reason he was required to report to the Paterson JCC was because he was a refugee and the organization was responsible for him and his family. He needed to check in with them regularly until he became a U.S. citizen. Rose cautioned him, "I just want you to know you're in America—you're a free man. You have to go by the rules. You were told to come here [Paterson JCC]. If you don't come, you make problems for us."

Abe read in his local newspaper that Rose recently passed away. She was also a resident of Fair Lawn and lived to be over one hundred years old.

———————————————

When Abe and Helen first arrived in New Jersey, everything was new and different. They needed to adjust to the American way of life including the food, culture, and customs. Abe tells a funny story of venturing into a supermarket for the first time:

"In Paterson, three blocks from my home, there was a big ShopRite. I had never seen anything like it before. In Europe they had little stores. Here, there were thousands of different foods. After what I had been through, this was heaven. The first time I went there I bought a [loaf of] white bread and brought it home. Helen and I didn't know what it was. It was soft and white so we thought it must be some sort of cake. We were used to corn bread and homemade breads."

In order to assimilate, one of the first things Abe and Helen needed to do was learn the language. It was far easier for Abe because he could go to school while Helen stayed home to care for Jack. But Helen wanted to learn English too.

"I went to school at night to learn English. Helen had the baby so she couldn't go, so volunteers went to our house one hour a week [to teach her English]."

Abe still has the original, heavily-aged, black and white composition book which Helen used over sixty years ago to learn English. The pages are brittle with yellowed edges but the words which Helen penciled in are perfectly clear. She wrote each word in painstakingly neat script and repeated it at least five times. Her lesson book begins with the days of the week then continues with sewing related words such as "pin," "button," "needles," and "table."

Besides learning the English language, the Pik family derived an additional benefit from Helen's home schooling. Through her English tutor, Abe received a personal referral for a job which ended up being his livelihood.

"The teacher—a Paterson JCC volunteer—that came to teach Helen English told me, 'My husband has an upholstery factory … why don't you go down?' I worked for that man—Mr. Solonch—for twenty years. When he died, his son Bernie wanted to pack up the business and move to Florida. I approached him and said, 'I want the business.' He looked at me and said, 'What are you *meshugge* [meaning "crazy" in Yiddish]? Where are you going to get money from? Half a million dollars?' I said, 'It's America. Do you need money? I get you an IOU—a mortgage.'"

It was an extremely gutsy move for a poor immigrant, but Abe was a fighter and purchased the upholstery business. He had a difficult time at first, but he persevered and ultimately turned it around into a very successful venture.

"I went in with practically no money. I was working twenty years in upholstery. I was a cushion filler, a springer, an outsider [finishing the exterior of furniture], then I became an upholsterer. I knew the trade inside and out. But when I got the business it was too much for me. I couldn't handle it. I wanted a partner. One guy I knew, a salesman/decorator, said to me, 'You're way too nice, you're not going to make it.' I didn't know I had it in me, that I'm capable. I got my schooling from the street. In Polish there's a saying, 'Necessity is the thing of life.' If you need it, you have to get it. I didn't have anybody here. Everything I got I worked for it and I made it. I'm sharing now."

Abe's upscale furniture was so high-end that his showroom was not open to the public. He worked directly with designers.

"I dealt only with decorators. People liked me. I was making the frames for the furniture. Until today I still see people that have my furniture and I'm over twenty years retired."

He proudly relates some of the places which exhibited his furnishings: "I worked with professional designers. I made the furniture on the bema [podium] at Fair Lawn Jewish Center. I made the furniture for a whole palace for a prince [Prince Faisal] who was secretary of state in Saudi Arabia. He came with body guards. I had lunch with him."

Being so successful and well-known in the custom furniture business got Abe's products into the homes of some famous Americans as well. For instance, he created a set of French Provincial chairs for Ted Kennedy with fabric a decorator brought over from Italy. He also crafted a house full of furnishings for Kathie Lee Johnson—now known as Kathie Lee Gifford. In a folder of treasured documents, he still possesses a handwritten thank you letter from Kathie Lee which she mailed to him decades ago.

Another benefit to Abe's success in the furniture industry was the special connections he made. He has a particularly fond memory of touring a famous Yankee baseball player's home.

"I was in Yogi Berra's house in Montclair. One of the designers I worked with had decorated it."

Eventually, Abe took on two partners and sold them his company two years before he retired in 1990, at sixty-five years old.

In addition to the money he earned and recognition he attained in custom furniture production, Abe considers a large measure of his success in life the fact that he was able to purchase a home for his family here in America. For a man who came to this country with absolutely nothing, he went on to purchase a beautiful two-family house on a quiet tree-lined street in Fair Lawn. He loves this home and still lives there today.

Abe & Helen after moving to New Jersey

Jack as a young boy

Abe, Helen & Jack at Jack's bar mitzvah

Business card for Abe's custom upholstery business JALEN

jalen

CORPORATION

ABRAHAM PECK

Manufacturers of Custom Upholstered Furniture

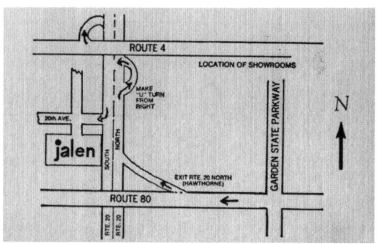

CHAPTER 23

Life In America

Citizenship

Abe learned that as a precondition to citizenship in the United States, applicants were required to correctly answer several civics questions about the history and government of the country. The U.S. Citizenship Test did not pose a problem for him. He proudly declares that he could easily answer all of the exam questions since he had been attending night school in New Jersey for six years. In fact, the citizenship process was so meaningful to him that he can still recite some of the questions he was asked over half a century ago. For example, one question was: "How many senators are there?" He recalls his answer: "There were forty-eight states at the time so there were ninety-six senators."

After narrowly surviving the Nazi genocide of European Jews, it was very important to Abe that Jack became a legal American resident as well. Since Jack was born in Germany, Abe took the necessary steps to ensure that he also achieved full U.S. citizenship.

"I'd heard that children born in Europe should have their own U.S. citizenship papers, so Helen and I went to Newark with Jack when he was six years old."

On a momentous day in October, 1955, after living in America for over six years, Abe, Helen, and their son Jack were sworn in as U.S. citizens. Drawing on his remarkable memory, Abe still remembers that the swearing-in ceremony took place on Broad Street in Newark.

In honor of this special occasion in his life, Abe decided to do something that had been bothering him for a long time: he used the milestone event of becoming a U.S. citizen to officially change his last name to "Peck." Although he was born with the surname "Pik," after he left the Nazi camps the Germans gave him the name "Pick," believing the "k" sound should be spelled with a "ck." Abe did not want to keep anything associated with Nazi Germany and permanently changed his name to "Peck." He kept in touch with a cousin in England who also decided to replace Pik with Peck.

High School Graduation

As an American resident, Abe was determined to finally get the high school education he had been robbed of by the Nazis. The only problem was that he was too busy with other major obligations in his life to give his educational pursuits ample attention. With a young family, a burgeoning business, and heavy community involvement, he could only devote an hour or two each week toward his goal. But this lack of time did not deter him. That same incredible inner-drive and determination that pushed him to survive and never give up—no matter how impossible the circumstances—kicked in again.

It took him sixteen long years, beginning his schooling in Paterson and finishing in Fair Lawn (where he moved in 1956), but at the ripe "old" age of forty, Abe proudly donned a cap and gown, marched down the aisle, and graduated from Fair Lawn High School.

Driving

When Abe first came to the United States at twenty-four years old, he was shocked to see that everyone drove cars. His lifestyle back in Poland and Germany had been rather primitive by comparison, and he was not used to a motorized society.

"In Europe they used horse and buggies. Some motorcycles, bicycles… a few cars. Here everyone had a car."

Seeing so many American drivers inspired Abe to want to drive too, so it was not very long before he set out to get a driver's license of his own.

"I saw an old lady driving a car and I said, 'I can do that too.' I got a teacher to teach me how to drive. Helen got a license too."

When Abe and Helen saved up enough money, they bought their first car. They had no idea what to buy, so Salah's (Helen's sister's) husband assisted them with this major purchase.

"I was here two, three years before I got a car. I had a brother-in-law, Henry Goodman, in Lakewood who bought up a chicken farm. Helen's sister married him after the war. He's gone a long time now. He got me a used car in Lakewood. It was a Chevy. A car then cost $400 to $500."

Uninformed Americans

One of the things which Abe found exceedingly difficult to accept when he first came to the United States was that the American citizens he met did not have an inkling of the horrors which Holocaust survivors had experienced at the hands of the Nazis. Even worse, the Americans he encountered were not at all interested in learning about the tragic plight of European Jews.

"In the beginning, we didn't talk about it. We all were like little kids. We didn't talk to American adults about it because they didn't understand. The American Jews didn't believe us … the stories about SS men, the way they pushed us into the ghettos, the way they killed us, the way they treated us. They didn't want to hear a word about it. It was too terrible for them to believe so we shut up. I shut up for years."

There is one particular conversation that rattled Abe over sixty years ago which still irks him today. He cannot help but grimace and shake his head while recounting the terribly insensitive reaction of one gentleman whom he had met in the park. After Abe had told him about some of the atrocities which had been committed against him and his family back in Europe, the man, seemingly devoid of compassion or understanding, turned to him and complained, "You think you had it bad [during the war]? I had to smoke Camels. I couldn't get a Chesterfield!'"

Abe estimates that it took between ten to twelve years—until the 1960s and '70s—before the younger people in America (whom he refers to as "the second generation"), wanted to know what really happened during the Holocaust. As more time has passed, he has happily discovered that the majority of people he meets are eager to hear true historic details from a direct source.

There aren't too many Holocaust survivors left, but Abe relates that there is a certain manner in which they greet one another. After the war, he began conversations with other survivors by saying, "My name is Abe Pik from Szadek. Did you meet any Piks? Anyone from Szadek? Where are you from?"

In America, he says his conversations always begin the same way: "What town are you from? Who survived from your family? What did you do here?"

Then the memories come racing back …

Long-lost Relative

Through a stroke of luck, Abe discovered that he had a great aunt—his grandmother's sister Yetka—living in the United States.

One of Abe's landsmen from Szadek—Felix Smietanski—whom he had lived with in Kaufering, Germany, after the war, had moved to Chicago. There, Felix met a gentleman in his shul who asked where he was from. When Felix replied, "a small town in Poland you probably never heard of called Szadek," the man said his brother-in-law Gedalie Hersh—Abe's paternal grandfather—was from Szadek. Felix then told the gentleman that Gedalie's grandson—Abe—was alive and residing in New Jersey.

As soon as Abe's great aunt Yetka heard the news, she immediately telephoned Abe (in Paterson) and grilled him on family members' names and trivia. Of course, he had no trouble answering her questions to prove he was really her great nephew.

In 1954, Abe, Helen, and Jack boarded a cross-country train to visit Aunt Yetka in Chicago. This was the first time Abe had ever met her, but he took one look at her face and saw the striking resemblance to his grandmother. She gave him the only photographs he possesses today of his family. These are the photographs displayed in this book and accompanying videos.

Students in English class in America

Abe's Certificate of Naturalization

Abe's Great Aunt Yetka (his father's mother's sister) in Chicago

CHAPTER 24

Restitution

When he was fresh out of the Nazi camps, Abe could not fathom accepting any amount of money as compensation for the murders of his parents, sister, grandparents, aunts, uncles, and cousins. But, with the passage of years, he was able to calm down enough to set his emotions aside and claim the restitution he was entitled to from Germany for enslaving him for five years and for killing his family.

However, as Abe discovered after he came to the United States, getting monetary compensation from Germany was not an easy undertaking. He had to apply, prove his internment in the camps, and wait several years before receiving anything.

He currently receives two pensions from Germany. The first pension was for the hard labor he'd performed in the camps and the resultant injuries he'd sustained. It took seven years after he'd arrived in America to begin collecting this pension. The second pension took most of his life to obtain.

"All the survivors got a pension [from Germany] but if something happened to you like if you were hurt or had a physical defect at all, then they'd give it to you faster or you'd get a few dollars more. I applied for a pension in the '50s because of my back so the German Consulate sent me to a doctor in New York. When I saw a doctor in Germany for my back after liberation, he said to me, 'You're twenty years old but you've got a back like an eighty year old.' When I started to work in the U.S., I had to wear a girdle with metal supports. When I became a boss and stopped heavy lifting, I did not have any pain.

"Starting in 1956, I was one of the first to get a pension [reparations] from Germany. It was very little. It was for the concentration camps for which

I worked and I am entitled to get through German law. At the beginning, I got $30 a month. Now, I get 579 Euros, which averages $800 a month. Helen got more than me because they recognized her ghetto right away."

By Abe's statement "recognized her ghetto," he is referring to the fact that Helen was in the Belchatow and Lodzer ghettos which were much larger and more well-known than his, so she received restitution for her time in the ghettos very quickly after the war. Abe, however, only recently began collecting restitution for his confinement in the smaller Szadek ghetto. This second pension for the Szadek ghetto took him almost sixty years to obtain.

"I fought for them [pensions] since 1950. They [Germany] said our ghettos [in Szadek] weren't big enough. They didn't give me. I asked for it, I was rejected. I sent them pictures. Finally, in November 2009, they gave me back pay for the whole time. Starting from 1950—it was only like ten dollars then—until today. I got one big check. The lawyer got almost fifty percent."

What does Abe do with his pension money?

"For me personally it helps me out. I live on a fixed income. Medications are a big part of my monthly expenses."

Photo Abe submitted to Germany applying for restitution
(Abe is 24 years-old)

CHAPTER 25

First Trip To Israel

After Jack's bar mitzvah on March 24, 1962, Abe traveled to the land of Israel for the first time. His wife, Helen, accompanied him on what was to be his first of seven trips.

Unfortunately, on this initial visit, Abe and Helen were not able to go to all of the sights they had hoped. Back in 1962, the capital of Jerusalem was still divided. Some portions of the city were governed by Israel and the others by Jordan. Thus, the couple was prohibited from going to areas under Jordanian control, such as the Wailing Wall and the Old City of Jerusalem.

As much as Abe wanted to see the famous Wall, he had to wait until one of his later trips. "It was guarded by Jordanian soldiers [during this first trip]. Israel got it in the Six-Day War in 1967."

Abe and Helen stayed with two of his first cousins who had also survived Hitler and emigrated after the war. These cousins, Israel Najman and Helen Najman Goldstein (along with her husband Alex), lived in Ramat Gan, a beautiful city in the Tel Aviv district of Israel.

"I used to be very close with my cousins. They came here, too, with their kids. One [of the kids] is a professor and one worked for the [U.S.] government."

Prior to his trip, Abe was under the mistaken impression that his Israeli cousins weren't doing well financially and needed assistance. Ever generous, he shipped over a large chest filled with essential items he thought they could use. But when he arrived, he learned differently.

"I sent by boat a whole big wooden box with socks and clothes. It was stuff for my two cousins and their children. But my cousins didn't want it. They were already okay. They had their own apartments. One was a carpenter, the other married a German Jew whose family had a factory."

Once Abe learned that his cousins were self-sufficient, he decided to donate his box of gifts to someone else who was truly needy and would appreciate it: his childhood babysitter in Poland, Hanna Nacha. It was her husband, Shama—Abe's Guardian Angel—who had saved Abe from death in Jaworzno.

"When they didn't want the clothes, I said I have someone who'll want it ... Hannah Nacha. She said she was very poor and had children."

Sadly, Hannah was a struggling single mother trying to make ends meet on her own while her husband Shama, believing she was killed in the war, remarried another woman, and moved to Italy. Unlike the disconnected couples in soap operas and movies who miraculously discover that their long-lost love is still alive and meet again in a tear-filled reunion, there was no happily-ever-after for Hannah.

Abe paid Hannah a visit during this initial trip to Israel.

"I only saw her [Hannah] once. She lived in Be'er Sheva (a desert city in southern Israel). She wasn't married. She must've been in her fifties. She had a job and I think she had some support from the country."

On this same trip, Abe also looked up one of his boyhood friends from Szadek and located him in Tel Aviv. Deciding to pay him a surprise visit, he hopped in a taxi and went knocking on his door.

"A few of my good friends went to Israel and survived the war. I have a picture of one—Libel Granas—he went to school with me in Szadek. His family heard that Germany took part of Czechoslovakia [the Sudetenland on the German border] and they went to Israel in 1938 before the war broke out."*[7]

---

7 In September 1938, British Prime Minister Neville Chamberlain gave the Sudetenland back to Hitler because there were ethnic Germans living there. This agreement, made to permit the Nazi German annexation of Czechoslovakia, is known as The Munich Pact.

Abe explains that before the war, most people in Szadek did not have the means to leave town and move their family to a new country. Even if they could have foreseen the ultimate fate of the Jewish people under Nazi-occupied Poland, they simply could not afford to relocate.

Moreover, getting into Palestine back then was not easy. Abe expounds on the difficulty of moving to Israel before it became a state.

"In the late 1930s, Britain would not allow people into Palestine unless they could show they could support themselves. The Granases had coal and a big backyard. They sold coal to people. It was a big business. So they had enough money to satisfy the British they wouldn't ask the State for money."

At the Granas household, Abe was greeted at the door by an elderly lady. She was quite shocked to see Abe.

"I knock on the door and ask her, 'Are you Mrs. Granas?' I told her in Yiddish, 'I'm the son of Yakov Shlomo.' She starts to scream, 'Oh my god I'm going to faint! I'm going to tell you, I was going out with your father. Your father's brother married my sister.'" [8]

After a few moments, Abe learned that Libel did not live with his mother, but she immediately summoned her son to her home.

"She called Libel and he came over. He had his own family. We were thirty-eight years old. I hadn't seen him for twenty-five years. He changed so much."

During his three-week excursion to Israel, Abe traveled the full length of the country, from the Golan Heights in the far north down to Eilat at the southernmost tip. He felt so connected to the country and enjoyed his visit so much that he returned six more times, for three missions and three leisure trips.

Bitten by the travel bug, Abe also toured many places in Europe, the Caribbean and the United States. Some of his most memorable destinations were the Greek Islands, France, Italy, Hawaii, Grand Cayman, and Mexico.

---

8 Both were killed in the Holocaust along with their children.

Abe (far right) in Israel

CHAPTER 26

Interview of Jack & Abe Peck - Part I

Abe's son Jack—born Jacob Pik in Landsberg on March 24, 1949—spent the first six months of his life as a German resident. He lived with his newly liberated parents in the small farm village of Kaufering until the three were able to secure travel visas to America.

Jack grew up in Northern New Jersey with all of the freedoms, opportunities, and privileges of an American citizen. He attended private school, earned a Masters (MA) in psychology, returned to college to study marketing and computers, worked for large companies such as Epson and Apple, and eventually started his own business in the social media field.

He met his wife, Susan, while on vacation in Grand Cayman, got married, and had a child of his own—David. Susan and Jack currently reside in a beautiful home in Montclair, New Jersey, not far from Abe.

Jack is an amiable fellow, highly intelligent, quite personable and very well-spoken. He is extremely involved in his father's life and is devoted to his well-being. He monitors Abe's medical care and takes him to doctor's appointments, makes sure he eats well, fixes his computer, regularly transports him to Montclair for dinners and family gatherings, and buys him appliances and electronic gadgets. Essentially, he takes care of all his father's needs. Recently, Jack's son David and his new wife moved into the top half of Abe's two-family home to be close to him.

As the child of two Holocaust survivors, Jack seems to have grown up largely insulated from, and relatively unscathed by, the horrific experiences of his parents. According to Abe, both he and Helen did not want to burden their son with the nightmarish details of the living hell they had endured.

Abe says, "We used to talk in Polish so he wouldn't understand. We didn't tell him. He was too young." Abe points to the Auschwitz tattoo on his left forearm. "When Jack was very little I told him it was a telephone number."

The remainder of this chapter is an in-person interview of both Jack and Abe. The interview begins with Jack's insights about growing up with two parents who survived the unthinkable:

> Jack: "When I think back about my childhood I don't have in-depth recollections. I knew about the numbers on my father's arm. I knew intellectually about what happened, but being an only child had a greater impact. Only in adulthood I saw some of the idiosyncrasies my parents and aunts and uncles had and how that may have been caused by the trauma. My mother would never ever talk about any experiences during the war. I knew not to ask her. It wasn't a topic open for discussion. Her sisters—my aunts—wouldn't either. My cousin Berta told me her mother [Salah] never ever talked about the camps."

While Jack is unable to specifically identify anything strikingly different about his upbringing than that of his peers, Abe recalls an incident that occurred when Jack was only seven or eight years old:

> Abe: "He came back from a birthday party from one of his friends where the boy got lots of presents from his grandparents. Jack was very upset when he came home. He said, 'Why don't I have grandparents?' I told him, 'They're up in heaven.'"

> Jack: "Not having grandparents wasn't something I was missing until I was older. I felt sad I had no grandparents when I was older. Growing up, I didn't have brothers, sisters, or grandparents. I had cousins. I went to Yavneh Academy until ninth grade. There was some education about the Holocaust. I

don't remember stories about my father until later on in life … college."

Abe has a slightly different recollection:

> *Abe: "When Jack came home from high school he'd ask me, 'How come you didn't tell me about it?'"*
>
> *Jack: "I really didn't start talking about it until I was an adult. Then stories came out in vignettes, piecemeal. The most touching one I heard is when my father and his father were in the camps together and they both got very ill and my grandfather died while my father was delirious and someone woke him up and told him his father was gone.*
>
> *"One of the things I knew about my parents was that they were strong. There had to be real strength there to survive what they did and come out and make lives for themselves. I admire their strength."*

Growing up, Jack seems to have only one prominent memory of his parents being unreasonable:

> *Jack: "My parents were very overprotective. I graduated from Yavneh Academy so I had one year in Memorial High School in Fair Lawn. I came home with a permission slip to see a Broadway show: Oliver. It was one month ahead and they said it might snow so they wouldn't let me go. I held that against them for a long time."*

Jack was a psychology major at Rutgers University in New Brunswick, New Jersey. He did not want to study abroad in Israel, but his parents were insistent that he go. His compromise was to take a summer course at Hebrew University of Jerusalem and tour the country. He was fortunate to have a relative—Abe's first cousin, Srulek Najman—living in Ramat Gan (a city near Tel Aviv) who had a son close in age to Jack.

Abe readily admits that getting Jack to embrace his Jewish heritage was a struggle.

> Abe: "Jack wasn't interested in his roots. David [Jack's son] is far more interested."

[To Jack] Did you befriend other children of survivors?

> Jack: "I had acquaintances whose parents were Holocaust survivors. My closest friends in high school weren't even Jewish. My parents didn't care if my friends weren't Jewish as long as they weren't girlfriends."

[To Jack] Did you ever date anyone non-Jewish?

> Jack: "I married a woman who wasn't Jewish and my parents didn't come to my wedding."

After a long, uncomfortable silence between father and son, Jack continues:

> Jack: "She converted and we made a second wedding, and then they came with their friends. The fact that they were survivors bought them clemency from me—the fact that they were broken and couldn't deal with this. My wife was very understanding."

Truth be told, Susan was more than a bit understanding: she converted to Judaism. After studying with a rabbi in Fair Lawn, she underwent the ritual mikvah bath in Teaneck to complete her conversion. She hadn't planned on converting at the time she married Jack, but Abe and Helen did not exactly take the marriage well.

> Jack: "They refused to even meet Susan. They'd say, 'I can't.'"

Neither Abe nor Helen could accept the fact that their son had married outside of their faith—not after everything they had been through.

Conversion was probably the only way to restore the fractured relationship between the two survivors and their only child.

> Abe: "I'm not religious, but I'm a Jew. I felt very, very hurt because that's what Hitler wanted, to get rid of the Jews. Intermarriage gets rid of Jews too."

> Jack: "We worked through it the first year. The fact that they were survivors was one of the reasons she converted. If it hadn't been for that factor, she probably wouldn't have considered it. Our son [David] was raised Jewish."

Abe speaks very highly of his daughter-in-law, Susan:

> Abe: "She's a wonderful person. She's like a daughter to me. Sometimes I say she's more Jewish than him [pointing to Jack]."

> [To Abe] Why do you feel Susan is more Jewish than Jack?

> Abe: "Because he doesn't care."

But Abe has a very different opinion of his grandson. In fact, when he speaks about David, genuine warmth spreads over his face and a proud smile crosses his lips:

> Abe: "My grandson is not religious. He's very interested in the Holocaust. In high school, he did a project about the Holocaust. I flew down to his high school in Texas to talk to them about what happened to me."

Irrespective of their differences, Jack speaks most admirably of his parents:

> Jack: "I'm very proud of him and my mother and what they've done. It makes me love them even more for being able to live their lives after … I can barely imagine what they've gone through."

Perhaps Jack's wife Susan says it best when she states: "The world is a better place because Abe Peck is here."

Abe & Helen (on right) with son Jack & wife Susan

Grandson David, Abe, son Jack

CHAPTER 27

Interview of Jack & Abe Peck - Part II

About Helen

Abe was married to Helen for fifty-nine years. Just mentioning her name or her sickness at the time of her death brings tears to his eyes. Helen had Alzheimer's for the last seven years of her life, and the disease grew progressively worse. One spring day in 2005, she decided to clean the outside walkway leading up to the back steps. Abe emphasizes that she did not have to do this, as they had a cleaning lady, but nevertheless she retrieved a bucket, detergent, and mop. Before she could begin cleaning, though, she fell down the steps and cracked six ribs, one of which punctured her lung. She passed away two days later, on March 12, 2005.

The latter half of the interview with Jack and Abe focuses primarily on Helen, her role as a wife and mother, and her relationship with her sisters. Like many other survivors, she was a hardworking woman who tried to live a normal life but was indelibly shaped by the horrors of her past.

Throughout Jack's childhood, Helen worked as a sewing machine operator. Instead of staying home, she went to work every day assembling girls' coats in a factory in Paterson, New Jersey. Jack begins by commenting on how his mother was a highly skilled seamstress:

Jack: "She was very, very good. She was very fast. She always under-reported the work she did because she was afraid she'd get fired. The work was piecemeal."

Abe explains: "If they worked fast they made too much money and then the boss would cut down the money. If they were paid five cents apiece he'd change it to three cents apiece. She wouldn't stop working. She loved it. She made friends."

Jack was fortunate in that he was watched by his two aunts while his mother worked.

Jack: "I spent my summers in Paterson growing up with Leo [Regina's son] while my mother was working. We also spent a lot of summers in Lakewood, New Jersey, with Berta [Salah's daughter] too."

Jack has wonderful memories of his time in Lakewood, back when it was all farmland. He, Berta, and Leo enjoyed carefree summers playing with chickens and horses, wandering onto fields, traipsing through woods. Jack spent the majority of his summers in Lakewood from when he was seven or eight years old until his early teens.

[To Abe] Did you and Helen want more children?

Abe: "No. It's part of my [lot in] life that he [Jack] is one. I came here penniless, no job, nothing. In order to succeed, you need money, so Helen went to work till he was ten. Helen had a better job than I did. She started off at $1.25. I was making $0.75. It took some time till I got going. Helen loved her job, she made friends. Even though they weren't Jewish— they were Italian, Irish—they were very friendly. When I got up on my job [was making a good living], she said, 'I don't want to go back to diapers again. Jack is already ten years old.'"

Abe further explains: "You didn't throw diapers away—you had to wash them. Helen had lost her engagement ring washing diapers in the bathtub. I had a plumber look for it but he couldn't find it. After five or six years I bought her another one—a better ring from my friend, another survivor, Motele Tropper. His parents were jewelers. He had a store in New York City on 43rd Street."

Like every couple, Helen and Abe had their differences, one of which was in their spending habits. In particular, Abe remembers how practical Helen was.

Abe: "She was a saver and I was a giver. For her birthday, I sent her a dozen roses. When I came home she was angry with me. She said, 'What are you crazy, out of your mind? Because we don't do those things.' But she was extremely generous with the children in the family."

Jack: "She functioned well, interacted very well. She worked for a long time. She stopped working when I was out of college."

But there were certain aberrant behaviors that Jack believes stemmed from her horrific past:

Jack: "She would say things to people that were totally inappropriate. I think of my mother as emotionally a teenager for all her life. Maybe that's what the world did to her—she got stunted at an adolescent age. She was a very simple woman. She was very funny … she had a loud laugh … very childlike in a lot of ways. There was an innocence. She was very loving."

Another common behavior amongst Holocaust survivors is the hoarding of food.

Abe: "She always grabbed food to take home. At a dinner party, restaurants, she would take food home. Especially bread."

Unfortunately, as Helen aged, she exhibited more and more signs which showed that her severe suffering in the ghettos and camps was still very much a part of her. Besides the physical manifestations of her time as a prisoner, such as the bad varicose veins in her legs, there was always the underlying internal anguish that no one could see.

> Jack: "My mother was extremely loving but she was a bit agoraphobic. She didn't like going out. She'd suffered great trauma. When survivors get out of the camps they make lives for themselves, and as they get older, depression and anxiety hits because they never dealt with it. My father wanted to travel all over the place and she didn't want to go.

> "She didn't like having guests in the house as she got older. When she was younger, they had card games. She was fine when I was little. Her main thing in life as she was older was David [Jack's son].

> "[In her advanced years] she became grumpier and less willing to do things. My mom was in the very early stages of dementia. She had phobic things, like she didn't want to cook anymore, which were not related to dementia. A neurologist did tests but it wasn't definitive."

Jack also opines that the trauma experienced in the war contributed to certain peculiar behaviors exhibited by both his mother and his two aunts as they grew older.

Initially, when the three sisters had first arrived in the United States, they were exceptionally close. Helen's sister, Regina, her husband Abe (from the double wedding) and their son Leo even lived with Abe and Helen until they could get an apartment of their own. When Regina bought a house, it was on 2nd Street in Fair Lawn, only a few blocks away.

> Abe: "Helen and Regina always stuck together. Their older sister, Salah, also moved nearby."

But as time went on, the close-knit relationship of the three sisters changed. Although they had jointly survived the camps and lived near each other in Fair Lawn, the trio became oddly distant as they aged.

> Jack: "The sisters hardly socialized. They seldom spoke. I interpreted it as they didn't want to spend a lot of time together because it brought up bad memories. My Aunt Regina was very depressed and withdrawn for many, many years—for as long as I can remember in my adulthood. She sat in a corner and read. She became Orthodox and wouldn't eat in our house."

Regina's son, Leo, presently lives near Abe in Fair Lawn and is a tremendously caring nephew, always stopping by to visit and help out his uncle. Every Friday night, without fail, Leo will show up on his Uncle Abe's doorstep.

> Jack: "My Aunt Salah [the oldest sister] was the opposite— outgoing and boisterous. She was great. She had a lot of good energy. But my cousin Berta [Salah's daughter] told me her mother never ever talked about the camps." After Salah's husband died, Berta moved her mom out to Ohio where she declined—Alzheimer's—and died."

In Jack's eyes, his father seems to have fared the best out of his closest relatives.

> Jack: "My dad is a high-functioning, mature, intelligent individual. He's very bright, very intelligent. In most ways, he's a very well-adjusted person. The scars on him are more subtle. But he's on medication for anxiety and depression—recently, from when my mother was making him crazy when she was ill."

Jack does not like talking about the Holocaust or his mother or father's personal experiences. To this day, he intentionally avoids Holocaust-related books and films.

Jack: "It's too upsetting. Most things that deal with the Holocaust upset me. It doesn't have to be related to anyone I know. There's a lot of loss."

But, despite his sensitivity to the difficult subject matter, he has managed to visit the U.S. Holocaust Memorial Museum in Washington, D.C.

Jack: "It was difficult but it was a good experience.

If Jack could deliver a message to the world it would be:

"Overall violence begets more violence. Teach compassion and generosity. Some people believe in the basic goodness of man. I believe in the opposite. If not taught to be civilized, there's no telling how horrible and barbaric man can be if the circumstances are ripe for it. It's a matter of work for people to be civilized. People are antagonistic. It takes a lot of work for people to act in good ways, to be kind and compassionate. The fact that my father is as generous as he is after the horrors he has endured is a testament to his compassion and humanity."

Abe, Helen & Jack

Helen (on left) with sisters Regina & Salah

Helen with Jack at his bar mitzvah

Helen & Abe

Helen & Abe in Hawaii

Abe & Helen with David

CHAPTER 28

Return to Poland

It took Abe sixty-six years to return to Poland, a land of heartbreak and loss. For most of his life, he had never desired to go back to the haunted place from which his boyhood had been cruelly cut short and his family senselessly murdered. Just the thought made him sad and angry.

But he was finally able to put aside his negative emotions when his childhood friend Joe Opetut, also a survivor, decided to restore and rededicate the desecrated Jewish cemetery in Szadek. In September 2005, six months after Helen had passed away, Abe finally returned to his homeland.

"I was depressed after Helen died. I never wanted to go back to Poland, but then my friend Joe called and said he couldn't find the cemetery."

When Abe first arrived in Szadek, one of the hardest things for him to accept was that there were hardly any traces of the Jewish existence he had known as a boy. Accompanied by his son Jack and grandson David, Abe drove through his hometown searching for signs of his prior life. Tragically, he saw that all of the beautiful structures from his childhood which were reminiscent of an active Jewish society had long been destroyed.

Pre-World War II, Szadek had been home to a thriving Jewish community. The town then boasted a magnificent temple named Bait Midrash, a *mikvah* (ritual bath), a *Hachnosas Orchim* (place for homeless people/travelers to stay overnight) and a *Gemilut Hesed* (bank known as a Hebrew Free Loan Association). Abe explains that the *Gemilut Hesed* provided interest-free loans to community members because "in the Jewish religion—in the Bible—it's a sin to take interest from others in need."[9]

In present-day Szadek, Abe was very happy and excited to see that the building where he was born still stood. He ushered his son and grandson inside and showed them the specific room where his mother had given birth.

Touring around further, Abe discovered that the quiet, small town of Szadek had radically changed since he was a child. It was now a busy, modernized city bustling with cars and crowds. The roads were paved and lined with street lamps, the sidewalks teemed with shoppers and pedestrians.

"When I left there was one car. Now there's no place in Szadek to park. Now part of the town square is used for parking."

He showed his family the big white pump in the town square which had provided the area's water supply when he was a child. Without running water, the townspeople had relied on a water carrier to deliver water to their home each day. The carrier had used a wooden apparatus he placed over his back and shoulders to haul the full buckets to customers.

As Abe wandered through the town, countless memories came flooding back.

"When we were kids, farmers came from all around and brought live chickens, butter, sour cream, eggs….They came by horse and buggies." He recollects women blowing the feathers away to see how fat the chickens were: "The fatter the better."

When Abe made his way back to his childhood home, located at "Warszawska No. 2," he saw that everything had changed. The small house—a one-story structure with a long street-side frontage—now had a gray cement exterior with maroon trim accenting its arched doorway and two windows. The kitchen had been redone and there was now running water. The finely polished wooden desk his father had custom built into the kitchen for his mother was gone. Abe recalls that his mother had used

---

9 It is significant to note that Hebrew Free Loan Associations are not just a thing of the past. There are currently over forty free loan agencies around the world. In fact, almost half of the states in the U.S.A. have free loan associations.

this desk to help others who were illiterate. Townspeople—predominantly women—had regularly come to his house for his mother's assistance in reading and writing letters.

Outside his old home, Abe saw children playing, which reminded him of some of the games he'd played when he was young. He explained to Jack and David how, as a boy, he had played a primitive version of baseball making bats out of branches and wrapping rags into tight round balls.

It's no wonder that after Abe had settled in America he became an avid baseball fan. He'd initially favored the Brooklyn Dodgers when their home turf was still Ebbets Field in New York, but after the Dodgers moved to Los Angeles for the 1958 season, he switched his allegiance to the New York Yankees who he still cheers for today.

Abe's love of American sports actually began with a humorous story. He hadn't been in the country very long and barely spoke English when he placed his first bet on a baseball game and accidentally won "big."

"When I first came here, I knew nothing about baseball. But when I worked in the shop in 1950, I won a pool betting in the World Series. I made only seventy-five cents an hour but won four dollars and fifty cents for the quarter I put in. It got me hooked. Soon, American kids were asking me about baseball players and scores and who was going to beat who. Until today, I'm interested in baseball, football, and basketball."

After decades of non-use, Abe's Polish was rusty but he stopped people on the streets of Szadek to talk. Most were friendly and enjoyed speaking with him. One elderly woman with thick white hair and glasses immediately recognized his name and said she had gone to school with him. He did not recognize her at first so she showed him her passport as proof they were the same age, as well as a school photo of their first grade class. She pointed to a slight little boy in the last row, second from the left, asking for confirmation that it was him. It was. And she was the adorable blonde girl in the middle.

Out of their entire class of over fifty children, there were nine Jewish kids. Only Abe, his friends Joe Oputet and Libel Granis, and a girl named Esther Mittleman survived. The rest were murdered by the Nazis.

During this visit to Szadek, Abe also met a gentleman named Wroinski who had been in the same school class with him. He told Abe that he had personally witnessed the liquidation of the Szadek ghetto along with the brutal beatings and mass murder of his Jewish neighbors.

"He saw them come with the vans. They closed up the ghetto. They took all the Jews. Anyone who resisted was shot, but first beaten bloody. The fire department came later to clean up the streets. He saw the people being pushed into the back of the vans, fighting not to go in. He saw how the exhaust pipes of the vans were turned to go inside and gas everyone."

Abe's jaw grows tight and his expression turns grim whenever he speaks of the Szadek ghetto liquidation because he is painfully aware that his mother and sister were among those forced into the deadly vans.

While most of the people Abe met during his return trip home were welcoming, there was one elderly gentleman who Abe recollects was not so congenial. In fact, this man's brusque manner immediately struck a raw chord with Abe, reminding him of the mean-spirited, hostile way the Polish people treated Jews when he was a child.

"One guy I met, he was my age or older, I said good morning to him and he gave me a dirty look and said, 'What do you want?' I said, 'I don't want anything.' He said, 'What are you looking for?' He was following me a little bit and then I walked away. I didn't want to bother with him. The rest of the people there were very nice. They were wonderful."

Modern-day Szadek

City of Szadek in 2005

David, Abe and Jack in Szadek Town Square at water pump

Abe's childhood home in Szadek

Old synagogue in Szadek

Szadek Cemetery

Abe's childhood friend, Joe Oputet, a resident of Long Branch, New Jersey, became a very wealthy man from buying chicken farms up and down the East coast of America. Abe recalls that Joe's father was also quite successful in business:

"He bought grain from the farmers and brought it to the mill where they made it into flour."

But Abe believes that Joe was an even stronger businessman than his father.

"He was a tough son-of-a-gun. When he had trouble getting a loan, he bought the bank. That led him to buy six more banks for a total of seven. He was the majority shareholder. He was so smart—one of the nicest guys if you didn't do business with him. He was so smart when it came to business … and he didn't have any education."

True to his roots, Joe Oputet was very generous to the people of Szadek once he achieved prosperity in the United States. He donated money to his hometown in multiple areas.

"Before the war there was one Jewish fireman—Joe's uncle. So he gave a big donation to the Szadek volunteer fire department. He also gave a large donation to the public school where we went on the condition that they teach about the Jewish people who lived there and the Holocaust. And they did."

It was Joe Oputet who came up with the idea of restoring the decrepit Jewish cemetery in Szadek. During the Nazi Occupation and the decades which followed, the Jewish cemetery had been grossly violated. Apparently, besides being vandalized and defiled, it had been so severely neglected that on a visit to Poland Joe could not even find it. He telephoned Abe, very upset that without any Jews left in Szadek to maintain the cemetery, it had all but disappeared. Then Joe decided to parlay his anger into something positive: he fully financed the restoration project over the next two years.

Not surprisingly, when the project was completed, Joe wanted Abe to see what he had accomplished. But Abe was reluctant to go: "I never wanted to go back to Poland."

Ultimately, Abe relented and when he did visit the cemetery, he discovered that two of his closest relatives—his grandfather and brother—now had unmarked graves. Abe's grandfather had died in the Szadek ghetto just before Abe and his father had been taken by the Nazis to the Rawicz working camp. Abe had helped to bury his grandfather.

"We got permission from the Germans to bury him in the Jewish cemetery. I know where my grandfather is buried, but when I went back nothing was there. The headstone is gone from my older brother [who died at two years old] but you could still see the foundation in the ground."

Abe knows exactly what happened to his grandfather and brother's headstones, as well as to the others which were missing:

"We knew who stole all the headstones. It was a *Polak*. He was a dog catcher. He put the headstones down to make a driveway on his property."

On September 12, 2005, the formal rededication of the Szadek cemetery was held. Abe and Joe, the only Jewish survivors left from the entire town, attended the solemn ceremony. They were joined by scores of local residents, Polish government officials and foreign dignitaries, including: the Israeli Ambassador to Poland, David Peleg; the Polish State Governor, Stefan Krajewski; the Chief Rabbi of Poland, Michael Schudrich; the Mayor of Szadek, Stefania Sulinska; the Catholic priest from the local diocese, and other clergymen.

"At the dedication the school kids were there with their teachers and they sang a song. The principal spoke too."

Abe proudly describes the improvements Joe had made to the cemetery:

"There's now a new brick and metal fence, a new metal gate with two menorahs and a Star of David."

A large metal plaque commemorates a Jewish community which no longer exists. There is also a plaque commemorating the deaths of the Jews murdered from the city of Lódz, where the Nazis reduced a prewar Jewish population of more than 220,000 to less than 1,000.

Presently, Joe Oputet is deceased and Abe is the sole survivor of the Nazis' near-total annihilation of the Jewish population of Szadek. He can only hope that the legacy of his people will live on.

Site of Jewish Cemetery in Szadek prior to Rededication

New fence and gate around cemetery

Back to Poland

Local resident attends cemetery rededication

Jewish Standard 10-14-2005

Lois Goldrich

Fair Lawn resident Abe Peck, born in Szadek, Poland, left his hometown at the age of 15 "as a prisoner."

"My crime was that I was Jewish," he added.

He returned to Szadek on Sept. 15, 66 years later, after five years spent in Nazi concentration camps and six decades lived as a U.S. citizen.

Peck, together with his son, Jacob, and grandson, David, went to Poland last month to witness the rededication of his hometown cemetery. According to the 81-year-old ... who, for many years, headed the Independent Lodzer Young Men's and Women's Society of Paterson — the trip provided an opportunity to visit the home of his youth and, by chance, become reacquainted with a former classmate, who not only recognized him but showed him a photo of himself in his old school yearbook.

Peck reminisced about life in the shtetl — Szadek had 500 Jews and even the Communists went to shul, he said, because "everyone knew what everyone else was doing and their grandparents would be angry" if they didn't go.

In August 1941, the Szadek Jewish community was deported to the Chelmno extermination camp. During last month's trip, Peck visited the cemetery at Chelmno, locating the section for those killed in Szadek, including friends and relatives, and paying tribute to their memory.

When Peck was first approached about the cemetery restoration project by old friend and fellow survivor Joel Opatut, now a successful New Jersey businessman and the driving force behind the effort, he was definitely interested but did not know what he would be able to do.

"At the time, I was devastated by the loss of my wife, Helen," said Peck. "My son thought it would be a good idea for me to do this."

It was at his son's insistence that he attended the cemetery rededication, and he's glad he went.

"There were Catholic priests, the mayor of the town, a real doll," says Peck, "other state and local dignitaries, the Israeli ambassador to Poland, the first secretary of the American Embassy, Rabbi Michael Schudrich, chief rabbi of Poland, and the chairman of the Lodzer Jewish community."

Peck noted that hundreds of non-Jews attended the rededication.

"This is a different Poland," he said. "People in their 50s and 60s showed me great affection, maybe because I don't live there anymore. Only one old man gave me a dirty look."

He said also that he whispered a greeting to the Catholic priest, who answered him in Polish, pledging to ensure that the cemetery would not suffer vandalism.

Discussing the genesis of the restoration project, Peck notes that Opatut, during one of his regular visits to Szadek, could not find the local Jewish cemetery. Going to the place he remembered, he found only an overgrown forest. Opatut resolved to restore the cemetery and involved both friends and family in the effort.

In cooperation with the Polish authorities and the Poland Jewish Cemeteries Restoration Project, which is based in Buffalo, N.Y., he arranged to have the land cleared, to have a fence erected, and to put up a gate and a black memorial plaque.

The PJCRP estimates that there are between 1,200 and 1,400 desecrated Jewish cemeteries in Poland, according to its executive coordinator Norman Weinberg. The group, founded about 11 years ago, has worked on more than 30 restorations.

Speaking at the cemetery rededication in Szadek, Peck said that "honor and dignity has been restored to those who are buried there. A plaque is there memorializing a Jewish community that no longer exists. An obligation has been fulfilled. A legacy remains."

Peck and grandson, David, at the front gate of the restored cemetery.

A former classmate shows Peck an old school photo.

Attendees at Rededication ceremony

Abe at Rededication ceremony

Abe and David

Abe with classmate from public school

Chelmno

On a cold and rainy morning, Abe traveled to Chelmno, Poland, the village used by the Nazis to dump the bodies of over 365,000 innocent men, women, and children whom they had ruthlessly murdered. Chelmno, approximately forty-five miles west of Lodz, was also the first location where Nazis used poison gas for mass killing operations—starting in 1941. In September 1944, when the Germans were losing ground in the war, they tried to cover up their crimes by exhuming and cremating some of the corpses dumped in Chelmno.

Nevertheless, in a mass grave somewhere under the vast fields of Chelmno, lie the bodies of Abe's mother, sister, grandparents, and other relatives. This is still a difficult fact for him to comprehend and he chokes up trying to talk about it.

"When you walk out onto the open fields of Chelmno, there's a plaque on a big stone about the 365,000 people. A giant sign [etched out of gray wooden slats] at the other end of the cemetery says in Polish: *Pamiętamy*, meaning 'We Remember.' There's a house—like a museum—where you can buy things. They give you souvenirs of some dirt. I brought it back and buried it here."

Abe stood in these sacred fields with his son and grandson and cried, saying *Kaddish* for his mother, his sister, his grandparents, his aunts, his uncles, his cousins, his friends, and all the others buried here whose lives were savagely cut short.

In reflecting on the significance of his visit to Chelmno, Abe references the teachings of the fifth commandment: "Honor your father and mother and you will be rewarded with a long life." But he did not have the opportunity to fulfill this commandment while his parents were alive since he lost them so tragically when he was in his teens. He never had the chance to show his parents how much he loved and respected them. Now, by standing on his mother and sisters' graves, to pray for them and to say goodbye, he finally got that chance.

"I was young when I lost my near and dear ones. But we grew up right away. We became men. I was sixteen years old when my father died. It's not like today. By us, they used to say you still wore short pants [at sixteen years old] … that you're not a man. We grew up in the camps."

This trip to Poland, filled with not only great sorrow but also with great joy, has left Abe more at peace. He treasures the memories of the family and friends he left behind. Now, most importantly, some of these memories have been passed along to his son and grandson.

Abe, Jack & David at the Chelmno Memorial

Chelmno mass burial ground

Abe at Chelmno Memorial

Pamietamy (We Remember)

Abe & David at the Chelmno Memorial

CHAPTER 29

Poland: Then & Now

Prior to World War II, Poland was home to the world's largest Jewish population. Polish cities, towns, and villages flourished with Jewish cultural, educational, religious and commercial life. Today, it is a giant Jewish graveyard; a country bereft of the benefits and contributions of generations of missing descendants.

The most promising aspect of Abe's return trip to Poland was that he did not sense the hatred that had been omnipresent as a child. He believes that the Russians who liberated Poland had a positive influence on the civilian population once the Germans were removed from power.

"It's entirely different now. It's my personal opinion that the Russians were there after the war and they taught them. When I grew up, there was antisemitism. You could touch it. You could feel it. One day a year—in the Catholic year—there was a procession on Thursday. They would break windows of Jewish stores ... throw stones. They'd beat up Jewish kids. The Jews ... we made ourselves a ghetto. We lived near each other. We had a big synagogue, two smaller Orthodox temples."

Abe was thrilled to discover that the citizens of modern-day Poland whom he encountered did not harbor the same intolerance and animosity towards Jews as their parents and grandparents. In fact, the mayor of Szadek— Stefania Sulinska—was incredibly gracious and welcoming to Abe and his family.

"I went to school with the father of the mayor—she's a woman. He [her father] was not my friend. He was antisemitic. She served us Kosher things and was so friendly. She sent me back a package. I sent her a Christmas package.

"The young Polish people are not religious now. I went over to greet a bishop. The bishop said to me, in Polish, 'What is your name?' I told him, 'My name is Abraham.' He said, 'Abraham was my father too.' He was talking about Abraham from the Bible. I said to him, 'So we are brothers. We should love one another.' He said, 'Yes, yes.'"

Documentation

During his trip to Poland, Abe was able to obtain important documents chronicling his family's history. One such document was the death certificate of one of his murdered relatives, his father's sister: Aunt Lieba Rifka Sara Pik.

Aunt Lieba was a young woman when she was killed. Lieba, her husband Prav, and their three kids never made it out of the Szadek ghetto. She was one of Abe's father's four sisters, all of whom were murdered along with every one of their children. Lieba's death certificate, signed by the Jewish leader of the ghetto, Chiam Beruch Most (the father of Abe's best friend, Monick Most), reflects that she died on April 22, 1942, in the Szadek ghetto. The cause of death: Rheumatism.

But Abe says that Lieba did not die of rheumatism: "She starved to death." He explains that the Germans would not allow the real cause of death to be stated on any murder victim's death certificate.

"Even if an SS man shot someone, the papers would say he died of a heart attack, stroke, or a disease. People who were shot, gassed, starved, burned, who disappeared … all records reflect other [natural] causes."

Other significant documents Abe managed to obtain from the Records Office in Szadek were the birth records of Jewish children born in Szadek in Abe's birth year, 1924, and in his sister Miriam's birth year, 1922.

The 1924 records show there were eighteen Jewish children born that year (separate records were maintained for non-Jewish children). Of those eighteen, only four survived the Nazi persecution: Abe - #13, Joe (Edel) Oputet - #18, Libel Granas - #5 (who went to Israel with his family in 1938), and Esther Mittleman - #9. Esther was also sent to the Nazi concentration camps, but Abe met up with her in the United States after the war. Esther's husband had a successful drapery business in the Bronx until the couple retired to Florida.

Of the fifteen Jewish children born in Szadek in 1922, the same year as Miriam - #11, only one survived the Holocaust: Eva (Chava) Smietanski - #14. Eva was the teenage girl who worked as a mother's helper for an SS man on the day the entire Szadek Jewish population was liquidated— meaning forcibly removed from the ghetto, murdered, then dumped in a mass grave in Chelmno. Eva is now deceased, but her husband, also named Abe, is still alive.

Another pertinent document Abe unearthed in Szadek was his parent's wedding certificate, still maintained in the archives of City Court. According to the official record signed by Abe's parents as well as several witnesses, they were married in a ceremony held May 7, 1918 when Abe's father, Jakob Pik, was twenty years old and his mother, Chana Najman Pik, was twenty-four. Rabbi, A. Morgenstern, signed the marriage certificate in court on August 2, 1920.

Aerial View of Szadek

Bishop and dignitaries attending Rededication Ceremony of Szadek
Cemetery – September 2005

Abe with Mayor of Szadek - Stefania Sulinska, Joe Oputet (to her right)
& Mayor's assistant (on Abe's left)

CHAPTER 30

Abe's Famous Cousin

Abe has a very famous first cousin whose original musical composition was recently given to President Barack Obama as a gift during Obama's March, 2013, visit to Yad Vashem in Israel. This talented cousin was murdered in the Sobibor extermination camp in Poland during the Holocaust, but the product of his musical genius lives on in many ways.

Abe's cousin is Cantor Israel Eljasz Maroko, the Chief Cantor of the main synagogue in Amsterdam from 1926 until he was deported in 1943. The original score is that of the popular Passover song *Had Gadya*—One Lone Kid—which has been sung at seders around the world for generations. Now, Cantor Maroko's musical creation is in the hands of the President of the United States of America.

When Abe was a little boy, he vividly recalls Cantor Maroko visiting his home in Szadek, Poland. The Cantor had married Abe's first cousin Rajsel (pronounced *Ry-zel*), the daughter of Abe's mother's brother—his Uncle Schmuel—when Abe was only five years old. He was too young to attend the wedding in Slupsky but remembers that Cantor Maroko had such a booming voice it made him run and hide.

Rajsel (Rachel in English) and Cantor Maroko had four children but only one—Simon-Wolf Maroko—survived the Holocaust. Simon-Wolf was saved by Christians and lived through the war in a nuns' home for children. Simon-Wolf came to the United States two years after Abe, when he was twenty-eight years old. Abe recollects picking him up from the boat dock, taking him to the airport and putting him on a plane to Detroit.

Simon-Wolf was not accepted into college in America, despite being very smart. Abe is uncertain whether it was because his English was not very good or because he was Jewish, but Simon-Wolf returned to Holland to attend college there for free. He continued his schooling to become a medical doctor, electing to go to Israel for his internship. There, he served in the military, met his future wife Ruth, and got married.

Ruth, a native of Poland, had moved with her family to Israel before WWII. Her father was a professor in Israel and she became a teacher. Simon-Wolf returned to Holland with Ruth but was ultimately convinced to permanently settle in America by Rajsel's older brother, Arje, the same man who had convinced Abe to marry Helen back in Kaufering, Germany. When Simon-Wolf finally returned to America, it was with Ruth and a baby boy. His new family settled in Michigan.

Simon-Wolf passed away a decade ago, but it was only recently that his widow Ruth discovered the story of how the handwritten score of *Had Gadya* had survived the Holocaust when almost all of the other musical works composed by her father-in-law, Cantor Israel Maroko, had been lost. Apparently, it took the publicity surrounding President Obama's visit to Yad Vashem to get the attention of a Jerusalem resident, Rivka Tucker-Aronson, who knew how the original composition had endured the war and made its way back to the Maroko family.

According to an article entitled "Vowing Vigilance, The Visit of President Obama to Yad Vashem" by Leah Goldstein, published in the *Yad Vashem Jerusalem Quarterly Magazine,* July 2013, Ms. Tucker-Aronson posted the history behind the survival of the work *Had Gadya* on Yad Vashem's Facebook page. Apparently, Ms. Tucker-Aronson's father, Aron Adolf Aronson, had been friends with Cantor Maroko in Amsterdam and was personally given the *Had Gadya* musical score by Maroko in order to lead a Passover seder at an old age home. Before Aron Adolf Aronson fled Amsterdam during WWII, he'd given his valuable items, including the handwritten sheet music from Cantor Maroko, to non-Jewish neighbors. When Aron returned to Amsterdam after the war, he retrieved his valuables and decided to give the *Had Gadya* music to the only survivor of the entire Maroko family, Simon-Wolf.

Along with the Happy New Year wishes Simon-Wolf's wife Ruth sent to Abe on Rosh Hashana in September, 2013, she also emailed him the *Yad Vashem Jerusalem Quarterly Magazine* article featuring President Obama receiving a copy of Cantor Israel Maroko's priceless work. Although Abe is quite proud that his cousin has been posthumously bestowed with global recognition for his famous composition, the attention also serves as a deep and painful reminder that his entire family was brutally and senselessly wiped out.

Given the popularity of *Had Gadya*, it is hard not to imagine how many other wildly successful musical scores this talented man would have created if he had not been murdered. And if all of Maroko's children hadn't been killed and they had gone on to have children, how many more exceptional talents would there be in this world?

These unanswerable questions only relate to the impact and influence of one individual. The incomprehensibly tragic reality is that the talents, contributions and creative genius of millions of people and their offspring, and their offspring, and their offspring, etc. are lost forever. For no rational reason—only because of baseless hatred.

Abe has another first cousin who, unlike Cantor Maroko, did survive the war. Sruleck Najman, the son of Abe's mother's brother, Abraham Najman, made it through the Lodz ghetto and Auschwitz, then moved to Israel. Sruleck's wife was the woman who had a nervous breakdown after the young couple had first emigrated to Israel when living conditions had been so challenging. She and Sruleck were the ones who had recommended that Abe and Helen go to America instead.

Although daily life had initially been very difficult for Sruleck and his wife, they ultimately decided to stay in Israel. Sruleck became a carpenter and raised two children, one of whom became extremely successful in academia.

Sruleck's brilliant and handsome son, Dr. Abraham Najman, not only received his doctorate at the Hebrew University of Jerusalem, he was awarded the very prestigious Aharon Katzir Prize for his outstanding dissertation. The results of his work were found to be of central importance in the application of the game theory to economic and political processes.

Again, how many outstanding, noteworthy, prize-winning relatives capable of changing the world would Abe's family have produced if almost all of them hadn't been murdered? Multiply that number by millions and the figures are too staggering to bear.

Chief Cantor Israel Maroko

"Had Gadya"

Souvenir for President Obama from the Yad Vashem Archives

Miriam Urbach-Nachum

media channels in Israel and the US. Following President Obama's visit, Rivka Tucker-Aronson, a resident of Jerusalem, wrote on Yad Vashem's Facebook page that her father, Aron Adolf Aronson (b. Amsterdam, 1919), was a great admirer of cantorial music and prayed regularly at Maroko's synagogue. The two men became close friends, and in 1941, Aronson was asked

■ *Avner Shalev presents President Obama with a facsimile of the Holocaust-era musical score as Prime Minister Netanyahu looks on.*

to conduct a Pesach *Seder* at the Jewish old age home in the city. In the course of his preparations, Cantor Maroko taught him the tune he had composed for the *"Had Gadya"* song, and wrote it down for him.

In 1942, Aronson and his brother managed to flee Holland. Before leaving, they gave many books and various documents to their non-Jewish neighbors for safekeeping. Inside a large Passover Hagaddah, Aronson placed the music sheet given to him by Cantor Maroko.

After the war, Aronson returned to Amsterdam and retrieved his books and papers. When he learned that the entire Maroko family had been murdered except for one son, he decided to give Simon-Wolf the precious score, the only memento remaining from his father. Aronson had committed the tune to memory, and every Passover, his whole family still sings *"Had Gadya"* to the melody he learned from Cantor Maroko.

Simon-Wolf Maroko passed away ten years ago. After Rivka Tucker-Aronson shared her part of the story, his widow Ruth and their children finally understood how the musical score had survived the war and found its way back to

■ *The sheet music with the composition written by Cantor Maroko in Amsterdam, 1941.*
Yad Vashem Archives

■ *Cantor Maroko, c. 1937.*
Yad Vashem Archives

their family. The composer had been murdered, but his music continues to resonate with his blessed memory – and represents a universal commemoration of all Holocaust victims, whose voices can no longer be heard.

The "Gathering the Fragments" Campaign is run in cooperation with the National Heritage Project at the Prime Minister's Office, the Ministry for Senior Citizens and the Ministry of Education. To donate Holocaust-related personal items so they may be preserved for generations to come, please call (in Israel): 1-800-25-7777.

The author works in the Teacher Training Department, International School for Holocaust Studies and in the "Gathering the Fragments" Campaign.

www.yadvashem.org for photos and video excerpts from the day, which were uploaded to the Yad Vashem website in real time during the Presidential visit.

President Obama at Yad Vashem receiving Cantor Maroko's composition as a gift

Original composition by Cantor Maroko: Had Gadya

Cantor Maroko's family wedding photo: Abe 4th from right & Helen
seated 2nd from right, Cantor's son Simon 3rd from left & wife Ruth to
his right; Cousin Arje far right

CHAPTER 31

Abe Now

"Here I am seventy years after liberation. I got a gift of living because 90%
of people [Polish Jews] didn't make it."
– Abe Peck, March 2015.

Abe is a remarkably astute and active man who recently turned ninety. His memory is perfectly intact and as the saying goes, he does not miss a beat. His body may be showing signs of wear and tear, but mentally he is razor sharp. Like the younger members of this millennium who are scores his junior, he uses a cell phone and spends many hours a day on his computer checking his email and surfing the Web.

He shares his gut-wrenching story of discrimination, captivity and overwhelming loss from the elegant dining room of his two-family home in Fair Lawn, New Jersey. Having spent decades in the home furnishings business, he is exceedingly proud of his custom-decorated interior.

In his living room, upholstered walls adorned with a swirling floral pattern of gold, brown and ecru perfectly match his large sectional sofa. Even the floor to ceiling draperies were designed in similar earthy tones to complement the room's décor and are made of the same fabric as the sofa's throw pillows. His hazel eyes beam with pride as he directs my attention to his master bedroom, relating how the furniture was created to match the upholstered walls.

Like the rest of his home, Abe's eat-in kitchen was professionally decorated. The bright and airy room boasts upholstered dinette chairs custom-made to match the cheery white and pink tulip wall paper. His beige counter tops are lined with all modern appliances. No matter when you stop by, you will find that his refrigerator and cabinets are very well-stocked.

"I have enough bread and bagels for three months. When I go shopping I buy it. When there's no more room in my refrigerator, I put it in my freezer. Food is sacred to me. That's what I got from the camps. When you go through five years of hunger…"

But Abe does not just worry about his own well-being. He is a deeply caring man who spends his time and money helping others. On account of the horrors he endured, he is not content to just sit back and let other people go hungry, even if they are strangers on another continent.

Several years ago, he and his family "adopted" an impoverished lady, Mari M., from The Republic of Rwanda. Abe fully supported the adoption idea—after suffering from starvation for so long in Nazi Germany, he has genuine empathy for those who need food.

He uses a few simple words to make a profound point: "Hungry people we should help. I was hungry once. Nobody should be hungry."

Mari has five children and was extremely appreciative of the financial assistance she received. Unfortunately, Abe's family fell out of touch with her after a few years when she stopped corresponding. Before she "disappeared," as Abe refers to it, she regularly sent him and his family heart-felt thank you letters. Here are two of them:

Letter I: "I was really happy because you wrote to me and that's why I also want to write to you so that I can get to know how you are feeling and I hope you will keep that up. My family and I live in Nyamata. We send greetings to you all. We have just started summer. We have a lot of sunshine. In our country they are harvesting millet and beans but I am unable to harvest because I was ill when they were sowing seeds but I was able to plant some vegetables in my small garden. I started selling goats whereby I buy them at a cheaper price and sell them at a high price so that I can be able to get some profit which enables me to pay school fees for my daughter. I do this on weekdays but on Sunday I go to church. I always pray for you. My children want to see you because you look good in your snap. They always tell me that they have gained another person in their family even though they lost some relatives in genocide. Let me conclude by wishing you good moments and I always miss you but that's the way it should be in this world. I am with you."

Your lovely one, Mari M.

Letter II: "I thank you very much for the support you are willing to give my children so that they may have the opportunity of studying like any other children. You have been both my parent and a friend. I miss my parents but since I got you, life changed."

The assistance Abe personally provided to Mari in Rwanda is but one small example of his unending generosity and benevolence. What is truly remarkable, in this instance, is that one victim of genocide survived to help make a difference in the life of another, decades later. All generations must recognize that genocide of any group, for any reason, in any location, wreaks havoc on our entire civilization.

Although it would be entirely justifiable for Abe to be angry, embittered, and lash out at the world, he has chosen the opposite path: He has spent his entire adult life performing community service and helping others.

He explains: "I do good things because bad things were done to me."

The deeper meaning behind this succinct statement is that Abe won his personal battle against Adolf Hitler. Every good deed on his part is yet another strike against his former oppressor. Every charitable act proves that he deserves to be here, that good can triumph over evil. No matter what atrocities were inflicted upon him, Abe kept his Jewish identity, maintained his spirit and returned to a full, meaningful life.

"The Holocaust made me a better man … I feel I wouldn't be as good a person [if] I wouldn't go through the Holocaust. I'm doing this when I give and I help people—and I do a lot of it. It's always that I'm doing it that I defeated a tyrant. It's another shovel of dirt on his grave."

Abe's lifelong commitment to assisting those in need is most notably demonstrated by his role as President of the Independent Lodzer Young Men and Women for over three decades—from 1972-2002. Abe describes this organization as "a charity that serves everyone."

"The Independent Lodzer made annual charity donations to dozens of organizations—hospitals, rescue squads, cancer funds, Alzheimer's research, child services, Holocaust memorials and museums—whoever needs anything comes."

The Independent Lodzer Young Men was founded in 1928 by Jewish immigrants from Lodz—Poland's second largest city, who came to the United States following WWI. Although Abe wasn't from Lodz, the existing members considered his Polish roots to be close enough.

"A lot of them were weavers, dyers and textile workers. When we came in 1947, '48, they were looking for new members. I wasn't a Lodzer, but I lived near Lodz. I became a member in 1950. I was a kid compared to them. They were experienced. When I became active they wouldn't let me go."

Abe speaks quite proudly of his lengthy leadership role in the Independent Lodzer. While he has derived immense satisfaction from helping so many people in need over such a long period of time, one of the recipients of his charity work stands out the most: an impoverished, crime-riddled town in Israel called Ramat Elijahu.

This town's inhabitants were predominantly poor immigrants from Bulgaria and Romania. Ramat Elijahu was in such bad shape that the Jewish Federation Services of North Jersey "adopted" the town and built homes, a stadium and a college. Abe personally pledged $5,000 in aid, then embarked on a trip to Israel to see the town for himself. When he viewed the dire condition of the community firsthand, he came back home to New Jersey and doubled his pledge. He persuaded the Independent Lodzer to match his $10,000 gift, and their joint donation of $20,000 went toward building a gymnastics center. A plaque commemorating this large contribution is permanently mounted at the new gymnastics facility.

Another major achievement for Abe while at the helm of the Independent Lodzer for Young Men was his successful campaign to end the second-class treatment of women. Until Abe's tenure as president, female members had no voting rights. They could attend meetings and participate in the organization through a separate sisterhood, but they had no say in the governance or operation of the organization. Under Abe's leadership, the name was formally changed to the Independent Lodzer Young Men and Women, and females finally attained voting privileges. This charitable organization still exists today, but it is not nearly as active.

At present, Abe spends his days attending educational programs at his temple, meeting with friends, reading books and online articles, and going on countless doctors' appointments. He still lives on his own, but does not stray far from home.

Although difficulties with his eyesight and hearing make public speaking appearances more of a challenge than in prior years, he avails himself of certain opportunities to tell his story. For example, one recent engagement Abe could not pass up was a Veterans Day presentation he delivered jointly with a Jewish American soldier who had liberated survivors from Nazi concentration camps at the end of World War II. Abe and the soldier each prepared videos highlighting some of their experiences at the time of liberation, and the audience was treated to footage of the contrasting perspectives of prisoner and liberator.

Abe is truly a remarkable man who, despite everything he has been through, still manages to remain genial and upbeat. He greets strangers with a friendly smile and hearty handshake, and those who are dear with a sweet kiss and warm embrace.

He is a lucky man who made a place for himself in this world when the odds were impossibly stacked against him.

He is a smart man who rose up from nothing to become successful in every aspect of his life.

He is a proud man whose invincible spirit carried him through the darkest of times and bleakest of conditions.

He is a charitable man who would rather give than receive.

He is an inspirational man who serves as a role model for anyone who has been abused, mistreated, or persecuted.

He is a survivor, and so much more.

Invitation for Abe's 90th Birthday Party

Organizations

Lodzers to Honor President Abe Peck

The Independent Lodzer Young Men will celebrate it's 60th Anniversary with a gala affair to be held on Saturday, Oct. 29, at the Fair Lawn Jewish Center.

True to the principles of the founders of the organizations, this fraternal group assists not only the immediate brotherhood but many other projects that it deems worthwhile.

After 7½ decades of extraordinary services, the Lodzer's have left an impressive mark of achievement in the community. They have funded: an ambulance for Israel, UJA Project Renewal in Ramat Eliahu, Barnert Memorial Hospital in Paterson, the YM-YWHA of North Jersey, Yavneh Academy, and the Max E. Bornstein Memorial Fund which presents scholarships to worthy youngsters. The Lodzers have strongly supported Israel Bonds, the United Jewish Appeal, the Daughter of Miriam Center, Heart Fund, Cancer Fund and many other local hospitals and institutions.

Abraham (Abe) Peck, the

ABE PECK

president for the past decade, has spearheaded many of these projects and has assisted the leaders and members to maintain the high standards which have characterized the 60 years of the organization's existence.

According to Abe Eisman, vice president, "Abe Peck will be honored at the dinner dance for his loyalty, leadership, inspiration and dedication."

Abe honored as President of the Independent Lodzer

Abe at 90 years-old in front of his home;

CHAPTER 32

Ask Abe

My initial question for Abe is one that has plagued me since I first learned about the Holocaust as a child—a question that no one has ever been able to answer to my satisfaction: "How could God have allowed the Holocaust to happen? How could God have stood idly by while millions of innocents were mercilessly tortured and killed?"

Abe looks at me squarely and answers:

> "Because the Jews were chosen to suffer! Starting at the beginning of the Bible, with Adam and Eve, Cain and Abel. One brother killed the other. From the beginning there was killing. God created people with brains ... they can use them for good or bad. Why pray to God? Will God help us? I believe that God helps those who help themselves.

> "I'm not religious, but I'm a good Jew. I was honored by my temple. I'm still a member ... I donate. The reason for taking care of one another is because when we were being sent to the slaughter no one in the entire world helped us. That's why when we say 'never again' it means we need to help ourselves and help each other.

> "What I saw, the hatred, discrimination, killing ... what was going on with no trials. I try to do the opposite. To help the poor, the hungry ... to be a good man. I feel I am a very good person."

One Holocaust subject that is deeply disturbing to Abe is when people criticize European Jews for being submissive and not putting up a fight. Abe finds it extremely upsetting when people ask survivors: "Why didn't you do something?"

> *"We were blamed that we went like sheep to the slaughter, but there was no way we could do anything about it. If you killed one of them, they killed one hundred of us. We did revolt, we did sabotage. There was resistance.*
>
> *"In the ghetto, in the camps, there were dozens of SS men on trucks and tanks with machine guns aimed at us. When they took fifty people [from the Szadek ghetto] to work there were twenty-five SS men, barbed wire all around. They had machine guns and we had to do what they wanted.*
>
> *"I read that in a town in the Ukraine in the early 1940s when the Jewish people tried to revolt they chased 1,500 people into a barn and burned them."*

To this day, Abe is haunted by the horrific years he spent under Nazi control. Beginning in Kaufering, Germany, he regularly woke in a sweat. The nightmares were more frequent and intense right after the war, but they have never gone away.

> *"I still have nightmares about being chased. When I go to bed, some things come back in my mind and I get it right back to all the good times I had in America. That's how I fall asleep. I had a good life. Being in the U.S. does not cure the pain. It made me a mensch—a good human being."*

Did Helen have nightmares?

> *"Helen used to wake up frequently from nightmares and wake me up … almost every night while we lived in Kaufering. She had dreams about her younger twin brothers who were killed in Chelmno.*

"We didn't have any therapy when we were freed. Now we could do whatever we wanted. When I was first liberated, I was wild—at nineteen, twenty years old. I would holler and throw things. I changed a lot with Helen and completely changed when I had Jack. I loved them ... there was life again. When Jack came along we didn't want to talk about it in front of him. We'd do things to remember our parents, our families. We'd have memorials."

What have you done publicly to keep the memories of your loved ones alive?

"When I retired, I made myself a commitment that now it's time to do something for my family which I lost. I speak in high schools, Jewish organizations, the Ys, Hadassah ... I'm being accepted very well. I was chairman of the Holocaust Memorial at Fair Lawn Jewish Center—it's a big wall made by an artist with all the names [of the victims] inscribed."

As a teenage boy in the ghetto and internment camps, you've said that you could never understand why you and the other Jewish people were treated so viciously. What were your thoughts at that time about the ruthless conduct of your captors?

"I'm a human being, how are they treating me like this? I'd think to myself. They treat dogs better. How can Jews be worse than animals? Now, when I see what's going on in the world, I think that people really are animals ... and it's not the Jews."

To illustrate the incredulity of the Nazis' butchery of the Jewish people, Abe recounts how he had a dog that became sick and to keep him alive he paid a fortune in vet bills. So if the life of a small animal can have such a high value, the question with no comprehensible answer that Abe asks is: *"How could they do that to a human being?"*

What was the worst thing that happened to you in the camps?

> *"Losing my father. Yes, he was one person—millions lost their lives, but he was my father ... a strong and healthy man."*

As Abe speaks about his father's death, his eyes cloud over with pain. Not only did the Nazis rob him of his father's life, they denied him of the final honor a child bestows upon his parents at the time of their deaths.

> *"How could a son not go to a father's funeral? Not know where he's buried?"*

Jewish people further honor their deceased loved ones—parents, children, siblings and spouses—by lighting memorial candles on the eve of the anniversary of their deaths, but Abe was cheated of this as well.

> *"I don't know my father's Yahrzeit. I say Kaddish four times a year when everybody does. It's a special prayer for my father."*

Some of the very last words Abe's mother spoke have stayed with him forever:

> *"'Remember,' she said, 'you are Jewish.' In America, I can say I'm Jewish and I'm proud of it. In Poland, my parents couldn't say that. I was sentenced to die because I was a Jew. I devote a lot of time for Jewish community work."*

What was your motivation to succeed in America?

> *"I wanted to prove to myself and the entire world that I'm a normal human being ... that I can be successful too. I am not worse than a dog, as Hitler said. I'm a human being. Being Jewish doesn't mean I should be treated less than a human. Every decision I made, I wanted to show myself and my parents that it was the right one—that I'm a good man. I have a lot of friends. People like me."*

Do you wish you could forget the horrors of the Holocaust?

> *"No. Sometimes I feel I'm not doing enough to remember. The people I lost are my family. I wish to make the world remember. I feel good about life that I'm still around and I can still talk about it. I want people to know about it. If I had knowledge to be a good writer, every day I could write a book about it.*

> *"I want to show the world that even a prisoner–someone less than a person, worse than an animal, an untermensch–I am not. I am a human being. They treated a dog better than me. When I get my freedom I can be just like anybody else. I can do the right thing. I can achieve things—and I didn't have an education. My education was in the camps. I try to help people. Survivors went to every country and were very successful. It shows life must go on.*

> *"The education I got in the camps, I don't wish it on nobody. What it means to be hateful is no good. We were hurt ... to hurt is no good. But we are fighters—like with sicknesses. We came to this country with nothing—no language, no money, no families to help us. Most of the people I know ... we made it somehow.*

> *"There is an old saying, 'Who is a rich man?' 'One who is happy with what he's got.' All of us had more here than what we had before."*

You did not hide, you did not escape, nor were you rescued. You were persecuted and imprisoned from the very start of the war to the very end. Do you think that distinguishes you from other Holocaust survivors?

> *"I try to bring this out with people my age. I was in the camps when Hitler was winning on every front. I was also in the*

*camps when Hitler was going the other way. When I first
went to the camps, some of the others weren't built yet—like
Treblinka. I was in the working camp—Arbeitslager—which
was worse than Auschwitz, and lost my father in 1941, and
people from the ghetto were dumped in graves in Chelmno in
August, 1942, when others [Jews] were still in their homes.
Hungarian Jews didn't know people were killed in Auschwitz
until 1944. All the people that survived came in 1944 from
the Lodz ghetto and Hungary. They were only there a few
months before they were liberated."*

Do you know any Righteous people who helped Jewish victims during the war?

*"Yes, I know of one, but never met them. The person[10] who
helped Eva Smietanski—the babysitter who was hidden by a
Nazi officer's wife when the Szadek ghetto was liquidated. Eva
came to America, married and lived in New Jersey. Later on
in life, she brought over [from Poland to America] the person
who helped her."*

Did you ever take revenge on anyone who brutalized you during your captivity?

*"There was a Jewish Kapo, his first name was Bolek. He
hollered and kicked me in the behind into the mud. I met him
after the war. It was a few months later at a soccer game in
Landsberg when the DP camps were playing each other. He
remembered me and went to shake my hand. I stepped away
from him and hollered in Yiddish, 'Let other hands do justice
to you!' I heard he went back to Poland, and there, a group of*

---

10 The Catholic woman who saved Eva Smietanski is named Malgorzata Podeszwowa.
Honored by the State of Israel, she has a permanent place in Jerusalem at Yad Vashem
on the Wall of Honor in the Righteous Among The Nations, her date of recognition
22/10/1981.

guys who were prisoners from the camps recognized him and killed him in Lodz."

How do you keep the trauma of the past from invading the present?

I live with it. I have no choice. Hitler learned how to hate and kill. If I would be like that I'd give him another victory. My mother and father taught me as a boy to be nice and respect people. I feel now this is the right way. To be nice cost no money. I don't insult anyone.

"I lay in bed and I say to myself, what are you complaining about? You got to live another seventy years. You have a son and grandson, you made a lot of friends, you have a house, people like you, they respect you.

"I have a dark side that I always remember but when I go to sleep I always look at the bright side of things. I think of the good part of my life. A few years ago, I went with my whole family to Sicily. With my wife I went to Israel and Hawaii.

"I try to act like a normal human being. It's not easy. I cannot talk for all of the survivors. Some didn't make it. Some went crazy. If I was mentally involved with the camps I couldn't run a shop or do things like that. Now that I'm retired, I have more time to think about it. When I'm alone, what do I have to do? I don't have Helen. What is there for me? I think about the past."

Do you know of any Holocaust survivors who committed suicide?

"Not personally. I only saw one prisoner at Auschwitz throw himself on barbed wire. A lot of suicides they committed by just giving up. After the war I know of no one who killed themselves."

Have you ever had survivor's guilt?

> *"I have it until today. I survived because I was lucky. I don't dwell on it, but it's still with me. Why me? Why my mother?" He shakes his head, visibly distressed. "She was just in her forties. And my sister? If I would have my sister … my god. I would do anything for her."*

What do you have to say to those who deny that Jews were gassed by the Nazis?

> *"I saw the gas chambers … the tall chimneys … smelled the burning flesh. I spread the ashes from there. I went into one after we were liberated. The parts of the machines were still there."*

Do you boycott German products?

> *"When my son Jack made money and bought a car he came home with an Audi. I wouldn't go in it for a couple of years. But now, I don't boycott German products. There are very few people alive who did what they did to us. The second and third generations have taken over and are running the places."*

In light of the horrors you experienced during the war, how do you handle funerals and wakes?

> *"The SS men were always beating and killing and shooting. We lived with dead bodies. At a funeral, I don't go in to see the body because there [in Nazi prison camps and trains] I was sitting on them."*

Do you watch anything violent for entertainment?

"I do not like violent movies. Things come back and make me upset to watch about the Holocaust. I try to speak up about it so other people should know."

What is your view on war?

"I thought this [WWII] would be the last war, but look at today. I can't understand what's happening. There's still hatred of Jews—a war against faith—but when people need us we help them. We are there. I give a lot of charity to non-Jewish organizations, hospitals, children, Jerry Lewis... I do know that if you do good, it comes back to you—bigger.

"I hope and pray that we never see again what I went through ... losing my family and friends. I say Hitler lost the Second World War, but he won the war against the Jews."

What do you consider to be your greatest accomplishment?

"My greatest accomplishment I feel is to have a child. To bring a child into this world. After what I went through, and I think I'm speaking for most survivors, is that we could bring children into this world."

Abe after the war in Kaufering

Abe today with his cover photo

Abe at his home in 2015

"Whoever destroys a soul, it is considered as if he destroyed an entire world. And whoever saves a life, it is considered as if he saved an entire world."

– The Talmud

APPENDIX A

Abe's Speech in 1985 as Chairman of the Holocaust Memorial Committee at Fair Lawn Jewish Center permanently hanging a memorial plaque:

In the last few years we have seen a miraculous growth of awareness of the Holocaust. Years ago survivors were considered refugees, few would listen to our story. Now we witness gathering of thousands, publication of important books and teachings of the Holocaust in high schools and universities.

On April 13, 1983, during the Survivors Gathering in Washington, D.C., Vice President George Bush formally turned over a symbolic key to the U.S. Holocaust Memorial Museum to Committee Chairman Elie Weisel. At that time Elie Weisel said, and I quote, "In building this museum we feel we have accomplished a mission the victims have assigned us, to collect memories and tears, fragments of fire and sorrow, tales of despair and defiance, and names, above all, names."

Each year when the world celebrates the end of World War II, we the survivors of the "War Against The Jews" think of our Jewish world that was cut down, of Jewish suffering and resistance. We remember above all our loved ones and the six million who perished.

We carry their memory with us wherever we go. We search for ways to inscribe it into the consciousness of our people and the world around us so that the twisted minds of Nazi historians should not dishonor their memory.

We the survivors who came back from the pit of Hell bear witness as long as we are here.

We must remember so that others are not allowed to forget. We transmit our memories of pain and suffering to our children, because we believe that by remembering the past we can build a better future.

Children of survivors, your task is to preserve the legacy given in Jerusalem in 1980 and re-affirmed in Washington in 1983, to remember and to warn the world that **Jews will never again be silent in the face of persecution and threats of annihilation**. Therefore, we want our national leaders whom we respect and admire to know that we are hurt and angered when they suggest that now is the time to forget.

We cannot and we will not forget the atrocities of that time. Nor shall we forget the American soldiers who died to defeat the Nazis. We shall never forget that America offered us a home and haven and became for all of us a land of opportunity.

Remembrance means keeping memories alive, guarding against denials, retractions and defamation of our experience. Remembrance means to preserve the memory of the six million Jews murdered in the Holocaust. Remembrance means commitments to the spiritual values of our perished loved ones, to recall the cultural, social and religious richness of Jewish life in Europe prior to the Holocaust.

Remembrance means *action*, to translate commitment into practical deeds, to work for the good and welfare of our people, with the State of Israel as its center. **Israel, the cherished dream of the six million which they did not live to see become a reality.**

By erecting this memorial plaque, we the survivors and the Fair Lawn Jewish Center have done something to perpetuate the memory, the story, and the lessons of the Holocaust.

In building this memorial, we the survivors feel we have accomplished one of the missions the victims have assigned us, to preserve

the memory of our loved ones and to symbolize that we, our children and our children's children will always remember.

Zachar, Gedenk, Remember.

"We cannot solve our problems with the same thinking we used when we created them."

– Albert Einstein

APPENDIX B

Abe's Message Today

I have a duty to let people know what happened. I want future generations to remember. I try to leave something that I did for humankind. Not just the Holocaust, which is very important to me, but also what I did against discrimination and hatred—the whole world has these. By reading this, I hope people will understand. There is no winner in war. Even the winner is a loser.

Hitler won the war against the Jews–he killed over six million. But he lost the war [WWII]. Over sixty million people died in World War II. Half a million Americans ... twenty million Russians. For what???

There's always someone that hates us [the Jews]. Before Hitler there was the Russians– the pogroms, before the Russians there were the Romans, the Greeks....

With all my past, I look to the future and I cannot see that I will have a good future because of all the hatred in this world. If people learn from the past ... what hate can do. But humans don't want to learn. Hatred can only be cured by education.

The Holocaust gave me a lot of things you should not do. You should not hate, discriminate. Be a good human being. Help one another. Help people in need.

For people who suffer, you have a second chance. Don't give up.

"I swore never to be silent whenever and wherever human beings endure suffering and humiliation. We must take sides. Neutrality helps the oppressor, never the victim. Silence encourages the tormentor, never the tormented."

– Elie Wiesel, Holocaust survivor.

"For evil to flourish, it only requires good men to do nothing."

– Simon Wiesenthal, Holocaust survivor and Nazi hunter.

APPENDIX C

Author's Note

Why is learning about the Holocaust so important? Because genocide is not just a thing of the past. In the last century alone, dozens of ethnic, religious, racial, national, and political groups have been victims of genocide. In fact, the mere mention of the word genocide not only conjures up the Holocaust, but Darfur, Rwanda, Sudan, Cambodia, Bosnia-Herzegovina, and Armenia, to name just a few.

Unfortunately, in the present era, there are too many dictators with brutal regimes who tyrannize and kill to stay in power, as well as fanatics who traverse the globe terrorizing others. If there is anything we should have learned from history, it's that we must eradicate evil as soon as it rears its ugly head. If we do not, then tyrants like Adolf Hitler will pursue their own perverse agendas at the expense of humanity. If today's advanced biological, chemical, or nuclear weapons fall into the wrong hands, it will trigger the end of our world as we know it.

How far will evil men go? The Holocaust, 9/11, modern-day genocides, and acts of terror throughout the world have shown us how far. In recent times, we have witnessed the destruction of human life through the bombings of hotels, office buildings, residences, embassies, military bases, marketplaces, restaurants, marathon spectators, ships, buses, trains and planes. We can never become inured to the cowardly acts of violence that so depravedly obliterate human flesh.

What is the best way to ensure there are no more Holocausts or systematic mass murders? It is through education. Teaching history, tolerance, and the devastating consequences of remaining silent and unresponsive in the face of oppressive rulers who persecute, torture and kill the innocent. We must learn from survivors like Abe Peck.

Political leaders may disagree on their strategies and tactics, but they must be united in the common goal of preserving freedom and democracy. They cannot be bystanders to tyranny and oppression, for their inaction will make them passive accomplices. Passivity will be viewed by tyrants as a signal to continue with their brutality, the way the Nazis took the passivity of German citizens toward the persecution of Jews as an indicator that they could get away with implementing harsher and more oppressive measures.

But not all European communities stood idly by while the Germans tried to persecute and murder the Jewish people. Denmark, Bulgaria, and Italy were three European countries which actively resisted the Nazis' attempts to arrest and deport their Jewish citizens.

Through a nationwide rescue effort by the Danish government, police, and ordinary citizens, thousands of Jewish Danes were safely hidden or smuggled by private fishing boats to neutral Sweden. Due to the Danish resistance movement and rescue operation, Denmark had one of the highest Jewish survival rates of any European country. The Danes proved that regular people, working together, could resist Nazi antisemitic policies and protect their Jewish citizenry.

In Bulgaria, King Boris III, the Church, members of Parliament, political and business leaders, and the general population refused to follow the Nazis' anti-Jewish laws. Bulgarian citizens rallied across the country to persuade their government not to follow a Nazi order to deport thousands of Bulgarian Jews to concentration camps. The public pressure worked and the King canceled the Nazi deportation order. The strong and open resistance of the Bulgarian people achieved an incredible result: no Bulgarian Jews were sent to the death camps.

It is estimated that 80% of Italian Jews survived the Holocaust thanks to the humanitarian and heroic efforts of regular Italian citizens. Italians of all religious backgrounds put their own lives on the line to stand by their Jewish countrymen. They understood that Hitler's actions were immoral and they actively protected, housed and helped Jewish residents and refugees. The Italian town of Assisi sheltered hundreds of Jews, the Italian inhabitants near the internment camp in Campagna helped all of the inmates flee before the arrival of German troops, and Italian villagers, locals, clergy, and police throughout the country hid tens of thousands of their Jewish neighbors.

The countries of Hungary, Finland, and Turkey also took steps to protect, rescue and stop the deportation of their Jewish citizens. Unfortunately, the resistance efforts of these few countries along with some notable individuals were the exception. Most people did nothing to help the Jews and other victims of Nazi persecution as they were rounded up and sent to their deaths. Millions stood by, said nothing, and did nothing while their Jewish comrades and countrymen were annihilated.

Future genocides can be prevented if ordinary citizens stand up for what is right and influence their governments. People around the world must recognize when someone in power is a malevolent tyrant and understand the grave ramifications of allowing that tyrant to exploit others. Tyrants throughout history have exhibited similar traits, which include: 1) Targeting certain groups as the cause of society's problems and aiming to destroy those groups to "fix" the problems; 2) Preaching hate-filled propaganda to drum up support and solidarity, and crushing those who dissent; 3) Using extreme violence and brutality to achieve results. Essentially, tyrants are power hungry dictators who seek worldwide domination.

The civilized world must be united in its mission to thwart evil and preserve our way of life. It must say, "Never again. We've learned and we're never going to let it happen again. Not to Jews. Not to anyone." Sadly, the saga of Abe Peck and his tremendous suffering and loss is merely a glimpse into the depravity of mankind. Most of us talk about making the world a better place but that doesn't happen when we allow innocent people to be killed. Instead the world becomes a place that isn't safe or fit for anyone.

When atrocities are committed against any targeted group, we, as a society, cannot simply stand by and passively watch. Leaders cannot shut their eyes. Countries cannot close their doors. Citizens cannot turn their backs. Why? Because no one is secure. What tyrants will do to some, they will do to others. When the atrocities are allowed to continue unimpeded, the tyrants will become empowered and gain momentum, believing the world approves of their brutality. And when the initial targeted groups are all gone, who will they come after next? It could be you.

"Mankind is a single, large, universal human race (...)
[with] no room for special races."
– Pope Pius XI - 1938

APPENDIX D

25 Things You May Not Know About The Holocaust

1. World War II was the deadliest war in world history. The death toll is estimated between 60 and 85 million, or approximately 2.5% of the world population.

2. During World War II, approximately two-thirds of the European Jewish population was wiped out.

3. Adolf Hitler dropped out of high school at sixteen years old. He was poor and homeless for years after he was rejected twice from the Academy of Fine Arts, Vienna.

4. Hitler was sentenced to five years in prison (and served under one year) for his attempt to take over the German government through a failed coup in 1923 called the Beer Hall Putsch.

5. Although born in Austria, Hitler was appointed as chancellor of Germany in January, 1933, by President Paul von Hindenburg. Less than three weeks after Hindenburg died, Hitler proclaimed himself *Führer* (leader) and *Reich Chancellor* (head of government).

6. Hitler ordered the executions of dozens of political leaders in Germany whom he perceived as a threat to his power in a purge between June 30 and July 2, 1934, known as the "Night of the Long Knives." Under Hitler's direction, the SS and Gestapo (Secret State Police) murdered the leadership of the Nazi paramilitary group

SA (*Sturmabteilung*, or Storm Troopers), including the SA Chief of Staff Ernst Roehm—Hitler's longtime friend—as well as other political enemies.

7. In 1938, Adolf Hitler was chosen as Time Magazine's Man of the Year. In 1939, he was nominated for the Nobel Peace Prize by a member of the Swedish parliament.

8. Hitler may have been part Jewish. His grandmother, Maria Anna Schicklgruber, worked for a Jewish family at the time she became pregnant and the identity of Hitler's paternal grandfather is unknown. Hitler's father was registered as an illegitimate child.

9. To create a "master race," the Nazis adopted the practice of eugenics—the belief and practice of improving the genetic quality of the human population by reducing/stopping the reproduction of people with unfavorable hereditary qualities. But the Nazis did not originate this concept of ethnic cleansing—eugenics had been widely used in the United States before WWII. Out of thirty-two states, the eugenics movement in California—using forced segregation and sterilization to prevent the procreation of undesirable traits—was the largest.

10. Two United States athletes were prevented from competing in the 1936 Berlin Olympics because they were Jewish. Sprinters Sam Stoller and Marty Glickman were replaced (by Jesse Owens and Ralph Metcalfe) as members of the U.S. 4x100 meter relay team the morning of the race. Both Stoller (posthumously) and Glickman received the U.S. Olympic Committee's first Douglas MacArthur awards in 1998. Glickman became a famous sports broadcaster for the New York Knicks, Jets, and Giants.

11. In May, 1939, the S.S. St. Louis, filled with over 900 Jewish passengers escaping Nazi persecution in Europe, was not allowed entry into the United States under President Franklin Delano Roosevelt. After both Cuba and the U.S. refused to permit the

passengers to disembark, the ship returned to Europe. The tragic events surrounding this ship's journey inspired the 1976 drama film "Voyage of the Damned."

12. The Nazis were thieves who stole approximately 20% of European art. Through organized looting operations, they plundered museums, galleries, libraries, public and private art collections, universities, governments, religious institutions, private homes and businesses of hundreds of thousands of paintings, sculptures, drawings, prints, ceramics, precious metals, cultural, historical and religious objects, scientific and technical materials, antiquities, artifacts, coins, china, crystal, and anything of significance to the Third Reich.

13. The Allied armies established the Monuments, Fine Art and Archives (MFAA) Program to protect cultural and historic monuments, works of art and other important items from destruction and theft during WWII. The civilians and service members of the MFAA were known as Monuments Men (there is a 2014 film of the same name). Despite their efforts, thousands of valuable works of art have neither been located nor returned to their rightful owners.

14. The Nazis not only robbed Jewish people of their possessions, but also of their body parts. Gold teeth were extracted, human hair was turned into felt and thread, and human skin was made into lamp shades, book bindings, and other ornaments.

15. Researchers estimate that by stealing cash, bank accounts, art, jewelry, furniture, and property from Jewish individuals and their communities, the Nazis plundered so much Jewish wealth that it paid for at least 30% of the German war effort. The Nazis also confiscated the gold reserves of every country they invaded. After the war, huge stockpiles of gold were found in Germany, but it is estimated that half of the looted gold had already been sold on the international market.

16. The Nazis devised a secret plan called Operation Bernhard to destabilize the American and British economies during WWII. In a massive counterfeiting operation which utilized Jewish prisoners as forgers, the Nazis produced millions of fake bank notes and dollars to flood the markets and bring down the world's financial system. *The Counterfeiters,* an Austrian-German dramatization of Operation Bernhard, won the Oscar for Best Foreign Language Film in 2007.

17. Nazi doctors conducted gruesome experiments on concentration camp inmates, some of which included placing them in icy water for many hours, injecting them with live bacteria, gangrene and/ or poisons, exposing them to toxic gases, castrating and sterilizing them, removing limbs and joints then transplanting them onto others, forcing them to drink only seawater, and subjecting them to high-altitude experiments.

18. People of Jewish heritage could not convert to another religion to avoid death. Germans had to trace their family history to prove they were racially "pure." Only Jewish descendants whose grandparents converted to Christianity before the founding of the German Empire in 1871 were spared.

19. Hitler was merciless to those in occupied territories who resisted German rule. In December, 1941, Hitler ordered that those who resisted be arrested and disappear into the "Night and Fog." *Night and Fog* is also the name of a 1955 French documentary film on the Holocaust.

20. The Nazi regime kidnapped hundreds of thousands of children throughout Europe and the Soviet Union for "Germanization." The abducted children were taken to Germany, forced to learn German, had their names changed to German sounding ones, and were housed with new German families or in German schools. Those children considered racially inferior were sent to Nazi-German labor camps, concentration camps, or executed.

21. Three time Giri d'Italia and two time Tour de France cycling champion Gino Barteli singlehandedly saved hundreds of Jews from deportation and death during WWII. Barteli, a devout Catholic, secretly hid counterfeit identity papers, photographs and forged documents in the frame of his bicycle to support the Italian Resistance and to help Jewish people. Despite the risk of death to himself and his family, Barteli drove his bicycle thousands of miles throughout Italy to deliver messages and documents, contending that he was "training" when stopped or questioned by authorities. He also personally led Jewish refugees to safety and hid a Jewish family in his own cellar, but never wanted credit for his heroism.

22. Starting in January, 1943, Jewish resistance fighters in the Warsaw ghetto fought against the Germans to stop continued mass deportation of the Jews to killing centers. By this juncture, approximately 300,000 Warsaw ghetto inhabitants had already been sent to their deaths at the Treblinka extermination camp. When the German forces entered the ghetto on April 19, 1943, in order to liquidate it, resistance fighters fought the Germans for over one month in the largest Jewish uprising in German-occupied Europe.

23. In August, 1943, approximately 1,000 Jewish prisoners launched an uprising in the Treblinka extermination camp, seized weapons, attacked guards, and set buildings ablaze. In October, 1943, prisoners revolted at the Sobibor extermination camp, killed SS guards and police, and set the camp on fire. In October, 1944, several hundred prisoners at Auschwitz-Birkenau who found out they were going to be killed blew up a crematorium and gas chamber and killed several guards.

24. After the war, Allied Troops forced European civilians who supported or collaborated with the Nazis to view the atrocities they had committed firsthand and to help bury prisoners' corpses. In

France, women who were believed to be Nazi collaborators had their heads forcibly shaved and were publicly humiliated.

25. Allied Forces established the International Tracing Service (ITS) in Bad Arolsen, Germany, to investigate the fate of millions of people and help reunite families who were victims of Nazism. The ITS has 16 linear miles of shelving containing approximately 30 million documents for over 17.5 million people arrested, deported, sent to forced/slave labor, or displaced from their homes during WWII.

ACKNOWLEDGEMENTS

The author would like to gratefully acknowledge all those who contributed to this book, particularly historians Hanna Schmidt Hollaender and Michael Nolte, editors Azriela Jaffe and Eric Koch, photographer Paul Garjian, Bitcon Photo & Video Productions, the Peck family, the United States Holocaust Memorial Museum, Yad Vashem, The Fair Lawn Jewish Center, and the Jewish Standard.

A very special thanks to my family who has been incredibly supportive throughout this project and to every one of my friends and colleagues who offered their inspiration and encouragement along the way. It is appreciated more than you know.

CREDITS

Photographs:
Courtesy: Yad Vashem Photo Archives
Courtesy: United States Holocaust Memorial Museum Photo Archives

Articles:
Courtesy: Yad Vashem Jerusalem Quarterly Magazine, Vol. 70 (July 2013)
        Article photos: Yad Vashem Jerusalem
Courtesy: The Jewish Standard, "Back to Poland," Oct. 14, 2005

International Tracing Service Documents:
Umschlag Abram Pik, Dachau, 1.1.5.3/6820477/ ITS Digital Archive,
USHMM

Schreibstubenkarte Abram Pik, Dachau, 1.1.5.3/6820478/ITS Digital
Archive, USHMM

Arbeitskarte Abram Pik, Dachau, 1.1.5.3/6820480/ITS Digital Archive,
USHMM

Häftlingspersonalkarte Abram Pik,
Dachau, 1.1.5.3/6820482/ITS Digital Archive, USHMM

Transportlisten nach K.L. Natzweiler v. 24.10.1941 - 9.3.1945,
1.1.5.1/5288292/ITS Digital Archive, USHMM

Transportlisten nach K.L. Natzweiler v. 24.10.1941 - 9.3.1945,
1.1.5.1/5288372/ITS Digital Archive, USHMM

Zugang am 12.4.45 von Arbeitslager Schörzingen, 1.1.6.1/9915289/ITS
Digital Archive, USHMM

Office Card Abraham Pick, Archival
References/64900251/ITS Digital Archive, USHMM

Natzweiler Transportlisten Schörzingen, den 7 April, 1945, nach Dachau, 1.1.29.1/3131367/ITS
Digital Archive, USHMM

List of all persons of United Nations and other foreigners, German Jews, and stateless persons,
1.1.47.1/5169707/ITS Digital Archive, USHMM

A.E.F. D.P. Registration Record Abraham Pick, 3.3.3.1/68610032/ITS
Digital Archive, USHMM

Displaced Person card Hela Pick, 3.3.3.1/68610158/ITS Digital Archive,
USHMM

A.E.F. D.P. Registration Record Jakob
Pick, 3.3.3.1/68610188/ITS Digital Archive, USHMM

International Refugee Organization Mass resettlement to United States of America Sailing ex Bremerhaven for Boston, Mass. November 19, 1949, on USAT "Gen. Sturgis," 3.1.3.2/81665288/ITS Digital Archive, USHMM

GLOSSARY OF FOREIGN TERMS

Arbeitslager – Labor or working camp (German)

Bema – Podium (Hebrew)

Bierstuberl – Beer hall (German)

Blitzkrieg – Lightning war. Military tactic designed to knock out the enemy through short, quick powerful attacks (German)

Cheder – Religious school (Yiddish)

Chuppah – Canopy under which a Jewish couple stands for their wedding ceremony, symbolizing the home they will build together (Hebrew)

Daven – Recite prayers (Yiddish)

Folkstsaytung – The People's Paper (Yiddish)

Führer – Leader (German)

Gemilut Hesed – Bestowing Kindness. Bank known as a Hebrew Free Loan Association (Hebrew)

Gymnasium – School which provides advanced secondary education (Greek/German)

Hachnosas Orchim – Lodging for homeless or out of town visitors (Hebrew)

Had Gadya – One Lone Kid. Festive song sung at the Passover seder. Abe's first cousin Cantor Israel Maroko wrote an original composition for this song (Aramaic/Hebrew)

Hajas – Jewish social service organization

Judenrat – Jewish Council that was required to carry out Nazi directives against other Jews (German)

Judenrein – Clean of Jews (German)

Kaddish –	Prayer for the dead (Hebrew)
Kapos –	Prisoners who assisted the SS in supervising other prisoners. The official government term for prisoner functionaries was *Funktionshäftling* (German)
Krankenbau –	Medical facility within concentration camps (German)
Kristallnacht –	Crystal Night, or The Night of Broken Glass. Rioters destroyed Jewish homes, businesses and synagogues, and arrested, killed or sent tens of thousands of Jews to camps in Germany, Austria and the Sudetenland on November 9 and 10, 1938.
Lagerführer –	Head SS officer commanding a particular concentration camp (German)
Landsman –	Fellow countryman (influenced by Yiddish)
Mach Schnell –	Hurry up (German)
Maftir –	Concluding portion of Torah service on Sabbath (Hebrew)
Mein Kamp –	My Struggle. The name of the book Adolf Hitler wrote while imprisoned for treason in 1923 (German)
Mensch –	A good human being (Yiddish)
Meschugge –	Crazy (Yiddish)
Minyan –	Minimum number of Jewish adults—ten—needed for prayer (Hebrew)
München –	Munich (German)
Muselmann –	Prisoner who is near death (German)
Nafta –	Kerosene used in lamps and lanterns (Polish)
Pasiak –	Gray and black striped uniforms prisoners were forced to wear in Nazi camps (Polish)

Petcha –	(Also called "Jallia") Cow's leg that becomes the consistency of gelatin when cooked (Yiddish)
Polak –	A Pole (Polish)
Rebbi –	Teacher (Hebrew)
Reich Chancellor –	Head of government (German)
Rudolphsgrube –	Rudolph's Mine. A coal mine in the Jaworzno subcamp (German)
Schlepped –	Carried or dragged (Yiddish)
Schutzstaffel –	(Abbreviated as SS) – Protection Squadron. Hitler's elite paramilitary force (German)
Shabbas –	Sabbath (Yiddish/Hebrew)
Shochet –	Kosher butcher (Hebrew)
Shteiger –	Civilian non-prisoner who handled explosives in the coal mine where Abe performed slave labor (German)
Sonderkommando –	Nazi prisoners specially trained in the operation of the gas chambers and ovens (German)
SS –	See Schutzstaffel
Staatenlose –	People without a country, or stateless persons (German)
Sturmabteilung –	Storm Troopers, or Assault Division. Also known as SA and Brownshirts. The original paramilitary wing of the Nazi party (German)
Talit –	Prayer shawl (Hebrew)
Untermensch –	Someone whose status is less than a person (Yiddish)
Völkischer Beobachter –	The official Nazi paper (German)
Volksdeutsche –	People of German descent who lived outside of Germany (German)

Wasserschacht –	Water pit (German)
Yahrzeit –	Anniversary of the death of a loved one (Yiddish)
Zlotys –	Polish money